[H.A.S.C. No. 113–75]

PEOPLE'S REPUBLIC OF CHINA'S COUNTERSPACE PROGRAM AND THE IMPLICATIONS FOR U.S. NATIONAL SECURITY

_____

JOINT HEARING

BEFORE THE

SUBCOMMITTEE ON STRATEGIC FORCES

MEETING JOINTLY WITH

SUBCOMMITTEE ON SEAPOWER AND PROJECTION FORCES

OF THE

COMMITTEE ON ARMED SERVICES
HOUSE OF REPRESENTATIVES

ONE HUNDRED THIRTEENTH CONGRESS

SECOND SESSION

_____

HEARING HELD
JANUARY 28, 2014

_____

U.S. GOVERNMENT PRINTING OFFICE

86–965   WASHINGTON : 2014

For sale by the Superintendent of Documents, U.S. Government Printing Office,
http://bookstore.gpo.gov. For more information, contact the GPO Customer Contact Center,
U.S. Government Printing Office. Phone 202–512–1800, or 866–512–1800 (toll-free). E-mail, gpo@custhelp.com.

SUBCOMMITTEE ON STRATEGIC FORCES

MIKE ROGERS, Alabama, *Chairman*

TRENT FRANKS, Arizona
DOUG LAMBORN, Colorado
MIKE COFFMAN, Colorado
MO BROOKS, Alabama
JOE WILSON, South Carolina
MICHAEL R. TURNER, Ohio
JOHN FLEMING, Louisiana
RICHARD B. NUGENT, Florida
JIM BRIDENSTINE, Oklahoma

JIM COOPER, Tennessee
LORETTA SANCHEZ, California
JAMES R. LANGEVIN, Rhode Island
RICK LARSEN, Washington
JOHN GARAMENDI, California
HENRY C. "HANK" JOHNSON, JR., Georgia
ANDRÉ CARSON, Indiana
MARC A. VEASEY, Texas

STEVE KITAY, *Professional Staff Member*
LEONOR TOMERO, *Counsel*
ERIC SMITH, *Clerk*

————

SUBCOMMITTEE ON SEAPOWER AND PROJECTION FORCES

J. RANDY FORBES, Virginia, *Chairman*

K. MICHAEL CONAWAY, Texas
DUNCAN HUNTER, California
E. SCOTT RIGELL, Virginia
STEVEN M. PALAZZO, Mississippi
ROBERT J. WITTMAN, Virginia
MIKE COFFMAN, Colorado
JON RUNYAN, New Jersey
KRISTI L. NOEM, South Dakota
PAUL COOK, California
BRADLEY BYRNE, Alabama

MIKE McINTYRE, North Carolina
JOE COURTNEY, Connecticut
JAMES R. LANGEVIN, Rhode Island
RICK LARSEN, Washington
HENRY C. "HANK" JOHNSON, JR., Georgia
COLLEEN W. HANABUSA, Hawaii
DEREK KILMER, Washington
SCOTT H. PETERS, California

DAVID SIENICKI, *Professional Staff Member*
DOUG BUSH, *Professional Staff Member*
NICHOLAS RODMAN, *Clerk*

CONTENTS

CHRONOLOGICAL LIST OF HEARINGS

2014

TUESDAY, JANUARY 28, 2014

PEOPLE'S REPUBLIC OF CHINA'S COUNTERSPACE PROGRAM AND THE IMPLICATIONS FOR U.S. NATIONAL SECURITY

STATEMENTS PRESENTED BY MEMBERS OF CONGRESS

WITNESSES

APPENDIX

PEOPLE'S REPUBLIC OF CHINA'S COUNTERSPACE PROGRAM AND THE IMPLICATIONS FOR U.S. NATIONAL SECURITY

HOUSE OF REPRESENTATIVES, COMMITTEE ON ARMED SERVICES, SUBCOMMITTEE ON STRATEGIC FORCES, MEETING JOINTLY WITH THE SUBCOMMITTEE ON SEAPOWER AND PROJECTION FORCES, *Washington, DC, Tuesday, January 28, 2014.*

The subcommittees met, pursuant to call, at 3:29 p.m., in room 2118, Rayburn House Office Building, Hon. J. Randy Forbes (chairman of the Subcommittee on Seapower and Projection Forces) presiding.

OPENING STATEMENT OF HON. J. RANDY FORBES, A REPRESENTATIVE FROM VIRGINIA, CHAIRMAN, SUBCOMMITTEE ON SEAPOWER AND PROJECTION FORCES

Mr. FORBES. We want to welcome our witnesses and everyone to this joint hearing on the People's Republic of China's counterspace program and the implications for U.S. national security.

Unfortunately, we have some votes that are coming up, so we have got a little bit of a time squeeze. Chairman Rogers and Ranking Member McIntyre both agreed that we will all waive our opening statements. Anyone who has an opening statement, feel free to submit it for the record. It will be entered into the record.

[The prepared statements of Mr. Forbes, Mr. Rogers, and Mr. McIntyre can be found in the Appendix beginning on page 23.]

Mr. FORBES. The other thing is we are going to, unless there is an objection, reduce the time for our questions to 3 minutes each, because we want every Member to be able to get their questions in. Because, unfortunately, tonight, with the State of Union and all, we don't have a lot of back time after we get these votes called.

We are delighted today to have with us three very distinguished witnesses who are experts in this area. We appreciate so much your willingness to be here with us.

The first witness we have is Dr. Ashley J. Tellis, and Dr. Tellis is a senior associate at the Carnegie Endowment for International Peace.

Dr. Tellis, thank you so much for being with us.

We also have Dr. Robert L. Butterworth, who is the president of Aries Analytics, Inc. Do not shake his hand; he says he has a cold. And we are going to say "cold," but we have something, you know, that is there. But he has been very thoughtful in not giving that to us.

And Dr. Michael Krepon, the cofounder of the Stimson Center.

And to each of you three gentlemen, we thank you for being here. On behalf of Chairman Rogers, myself, Mr. McIntyre, Mr. Cooper, we thank you for giving us your time and expertise.

And now we would like to ask you if you could take 3 to 5 minutes to give us whatever statements you have. Your written statements, of course, will be part of the record, and we have read those already.

And, Dr. Tellis, are we going to start with you, or have you predetermined that?

Dr. TELLIS. Yes.

Mr. FORBES. Then, Dr. Tellis, we would love to have you start off for us.

STATEMENT OF DR. ASHLEY J. TELLIS, SENIOR ASSOCIATE, CARNEGIE ENDOWMENT FOR INTERNATIONAL PEACE

Dr. TELLIS. Thank you, Mr. Chairman.

Chairman Rogers, Chairman Forbes, the distinguished ranking members, members of the subcommittee, thank you for the invitation to present today on China's counterspace programs.

In the interest of time, I am going to keep my comments extremely brief. I want to make five basic points for your consideration.

The first point is that the current and the evolving counterspace threat posed by China to U.S. military operations in the Asia-Pacific theater and outside is extremely serious. And the threat ranks on par with the dangers posed by Chinese offensive cyber operations to the United States more generally. That is the first point.

The second point is that the diversity and the complexity of China's counterspace programs make them particularly problematic, because they span the gamut all the way from direct-ascent and co-orbital ASAT [anti-satellite] programs, which receive enormous attention, to equally challenging threats like electronic warfare intended to paralyze U.S. satellite communications, which actually get very little attention, to more recondite dangers, such as directed-energy weapons and radiofrequency weapons and computer network attack capabilities, which are rather hard to understand. So it is the complexity and the diversity of these threats that magnify the challenges faced by the United States.

The third point I want to make is that these dangers are acute because the U.S. space systems which are the targets of China's activities are simultaneously extraordinarily vulnerable and extraordinarily valuable at the same time.

The fourth point is that the incentives that drive China to pursue its counterspace programs are strong and will only intensify over time for the simple reason that China views itself as being in a geopolitical competition with the United States and believes that it must prepare itself for a possible conflict with a superior U.S. military. Given this perception, Chinese military planners are deeply focused on neutralizing American space capabilities because of their belief that such neutralization is essential to whittle down the information dominance on which the United States military depends on for its success.

The fifth and last point is a more controversial one, but I think I should make it. Given China's incentives and the reasons why it is pursuing a counterspace program, I do not believe Beijing can be dissuaded from moving in a different direction through arms-control agreements.

The only way to persuade China that its counterspace programs will not deliver the returns that it seeks, if there is any way at all, is for the United States to ensure that its military forces can operate successfully despite China's investments in counterspace. This will require, at the very least, diverse new kinds of investments, which are essential for the United States to protect its success in power projection operations that will be necessary in the years to come.

Let me end on that note, and thank you for your attention.

[The prepared statement of Dr. Tellis can be found in the Appendix on page 28.]

Mr. FORBES. Thank you so much, Dr. Tellis.

Dr. Butterworth.

STATEMENT OF DR. ROBERT L. BUTTERWORTH, PRESIDENT, ARIES ANALYTICS, INC.

Dr. BUTTERWORTH. Chairman Forbes, Chairman Rogers, Ranking Member McIntyre, Ranking Member Cooper, distinguished members of the committees, thank you very much for convening this hearing.

The topic is terribly important, the facts of the matter at hand are debated, and the consequences of the approaches open to us are neither clear nor guaranteed. We need a lot more attention to this problem to help shape our judgments about the way ahead.

China is a large, growing, militarily and economically strong assertive power. It has gone to war to expand its control over contiguous regions at least four times since the Korean war. It might well have done so again in its recent disputes with Vietnam, Korea, Japan, the Philippines, and Taiwan except that its demands now involve a region of national security interest to the United States and U.S. allies. China is not yet ready for a military confrontation with the United States.

If things go well, that confrontation may never occur, but China does seem determined to prepare for one as it seeks to exert unilateral authority over an ever-expanding neighborhood.

A bellwether here is China's experimentation with counterspace operations. If China can deprive the United States of reliable and timely space support, our force movements will be slower and less coordinated, our longer-range weapons less responsive and less accurate, our tactical operations in general less focused and more costly, and our global awareness more myopic and less timely.

China's most notorious counterspace experiment involved a direct-ascent hit-to-kill technology—that was in January of 2007—but it is surely looking at other approaches, too, as Dr. Tellis just mentioned, including other kinetic-energy weapons, lasers, jammers, cyber tools to attack data and command and control systems. For the near term, at least, I think it will probably favor systems to achieve mission kill by attacking U.S. satellites directly, either from orbit or from the ground.

China will also want to know what U.S. satellites to kill in order to achieve the desired degradation in U.S. military capabilities. I expect that targeting is a problem, and possibly the problem, that will be addressed using the sort of capabilities for precision orbital and proximity operations that China demonstrated starting a few months ago.

Such operations could help China characterize the U.S. space architecture and perhaps place sensors close to U.S. satellites that could provide clues about the how, what, and when of the satellites being used for military operations. If true, then we should expect to see more extensive examination and operational probes in the future.

So China still has some distance to go before it can be confident in a confrontation, but so does the United States. There are things we can do to protect some satellites against some threats: We can try to complicate China's targeting problems by exploiting deficiencies in its ability to detect and track potential targets. We can further harden satellite subsystems to resist thermal and electronic attacks. And we might find ways to engage and defeat an attacker's weapons before they engage our satellites.

But China's counterspace activities presents a broader challenge. To meet it, we need to know how to integrate space control into plans and preparations for the joint fight more broadly. Changes in our space order of battle, whether they come about through defensive movements on our part or attacks by an enemy or random mishap, can immediately alter the effectiveness of our terrestrial forces.

We need to make sure that command and control is unified and timely. We need experiments, demonstrations, and exercises that more realistically test our forces' abilities to detect, attribute, and respond to attacks on our space systems. We need to develop, execute, and repeatedly test plans for operations, particularly for power projection, when space is contested.

We need to better coordinate the planning and developing of space defenses. We need to assess the cost-effectiveness of selected alternatives to space support. And I hope that we can further integrate space into the joint fight by coupling space programs more closely with other force-development activities.

The perspective offered here, what I am talking about, is that the United States and China are in a long-term military competition which includes significant effort in space. This competition is not a policy of momentary advantage or a transient appeal, and it creates a core issue of national security between China and the United States. It is about and will require real capabilities. Finding ways to negate the U.S. military space advantage is a compelling strategic requirement for China. It won't be moderated by proselytizing space norms or deterrence by demarche or a code of conduct for good guys in space.

None of this is meant to suggest that war with China is inevitable. It does suggest that a good way to help China join and strengthen the international order is to be prepared to maintain American principles militarily, including in space.

Thanks for your attention.

[The prepared statement of Dr. Butterworth can be found in the Appendix on page 41.]

Mr. FORBES. Thank you, Dr. Butterworth.

Mr. Krepon.

STATEMENT OF MICHAEL KREPON, COFOUNDER AND SENIOR ASSOCIATE, THE STIMSON CENTER

Mr. KREPON. Thank you, Chairman.

Mr. FORBES. Mr. Krepon, you might need to pull that microphone as close as you can. It doesn't pick up very well.

Mr. KREPON. Chairman Rogers, Chairman Forbes, Ranking Minority Members McIntyre, Cooper, members of this committee, I have a huge sense of déjà vu sitting here, because I was a staffer for a member of this committee when the leadership was Mr. Hébert, Mr. Rivers, and Mr. Price, who are looking down on us now.

And back then, the issue was the Soviet space challenge, and it was very severe. And a lot of the capabilities that China is testing, evaluating, improving aren't new. Those capabilities existed back then, as well. And we had, as you well know, an intense nuclear competition with Moscow, an intense space race with Moscow. We had crises. We competed for ideological and geopolitical advantage. It was a fierce competition.

And yet the worst fears of warfare in space were not realized; warfare, terrestrial and on the seas, were not realized. How did we succeed back then in deterring a determined and highly capable adversary, and are there any takeaways for us now?

I think there are several reasons why we avoided warfare in space back then. One was that we couldn't firewall it away from warfare in other domains. The prospect of uncontrolled escalation was in front of us and in front of Moscow. Number two, the capabilities in space were so vulnerable that if somebody wanted to start shooting up there, we could both be extremely harmed. And, also, military capabilities that we had invested in and the Soviets invested in for other purposes could be repurposed for use in space warfare.

Now, all of these conditions are true today also, but we can't depend on them to prevent China from doing things that are extremely harmful to us. So we can't rely on these existing conditions to defend ourselves. We need a strategy to deal with very real threats to assets that are very meaningful to our Armed Forces and to our economic security.

So what do we do? One thing we can do is to increase the resilience of our space assets. We can do this to help deter or foil some kinds of attacks, even though our satellites will remain vulnerable to a determined attacker willing to suffer the consequences.

What else can we do? We can deter or dissuade through disaggregation, to the extent that we have the resources to do so. Deterrence of attack is increased by complicating the plans of the attacker.

What else can we do? Space situational awareness. The extent to which we can deter depends on how much we know ahead of time. And if the committee underfunds space situational awareness, then our deterrence capabilities can be diminished even if we are doing the other things right.

What else can we do? We can retain the capability to respond in ways of our choosing if somebody messes with our space assets or the infrastructure for our space assets. We have these capabilities today. They are actually greater today than they were during the cold war.

Now, do we need specific types of weapons that are dedicated to the mission of destroying, damaging, disrupting satellites? Do we need dedicated, online, ready-to-respond-quickly types of capability, like we do in the nuclear arena? In my view, there is so much latent capability to do this now, we don't need dedicated—certain types of dedicated capability.

I don't think we need the capability that messes space up for us as well as for the other guy. So capability that creates mutating debris fields, which are indiscriminate and long-lasting in their effects, it doesn't matter if it is your satellite, my satellite, somebody else's satellite, I don't think we need that. But we have the capability if we need to.

Diplomacy. You know, I think one of the lessons a lot of people learned during the cold war was that deterrence is stronger when it is backed up by diplomacy. Now, we can't do treaties in space, but we can do, I think, a code of conduct that makes rules and establishes rules of responsible, as opposed to irresponsible, behavior. Without rules, there are no rule-breakers. I think norms can serve our interests.

So I am suggesting to you, Mr. Chairman, or Mr. Chairmen, a multilayered approach to deal with a very serious problem.

Thank you.

[The prepared statement of Mr. Krepon can be found in the Appendix on page 48.]

Mr. FORBES. Thank you, Mr. Krepon.

Just to let you know and the people in this room, one of the interesting things about the Armed Services Committee, we are probably the most bipartisan subcommittee in Congress. The two ranking members and both Mr. Rogers and I have enormous respect for each other. And our Members here are all looking to find a solution, as opposed to just driving things politically.

I appreciate you coming here today and outlining what you think we should do. And in my 3 minutes, I just want to basically suggest—I think there are three questions we have to ask: One, what exactly is the vulnerabilities that we have? Number two, what is the magnitude of that problem? And, number three, what can we do to fix it? Because part of what we do with these hearings is try to take a message to our other Members to let them understand exactly what we are looking at.

Dr. Tellis, you gave us an excellent five-point presentation. Your first one is very concerning to me because you indicated that you view the problem as extremely serious and on par with the cyber problems. And most of us have some feel for how serious the cyber threat is from China today.

The question I would ask to all three of you is, assume this happens. Give us your picture of the vulnerabilities that we have and then what exactly it would do to us from a capability point of view. And, if you can, give us what specificity you can give us, as opposed to just globally, you know, hitting in there.

Dr. Tellis, do you mind starting off with that? And then I would love to have each one of you weigh in.

Dr. TELLIS. I think there are two capabilities that the Chinese have invested in which pose specific kinds of threats.

The kinetic kill capabilities obviously have a specific effect on low-Earth-orbit satellites. And, obviously, the key satellites there that matter are electro-optical surveillance satellites, which are most at risk because you can interfere with their operations not simply through kinetic kill but through laser dazzling and so on and so forth. So even if you don't get hard kills that contribute to the debris that Mr. Krepon has correctly identified is a serious challenge, you can interfere with their operation through directed-energy devices, which China has been pursuing for the last several years.

The second issue which I think bears on the magnitude-of-vulnerability question, which I am concerned about, has to do with U.S. communications satellites, because China has made enormous investments in jamming. And there are a class of U.S. communication satellites which are protected, which are going to be more impervious to the Chinese capabilities that are coming on line, but much of our warfighting efficiency depends on being able to use commercial satellites and other kinds of military satellites which are unprotected.

And I think if we lose the capacity embodied in those unprotected assets, then, of necessity, the burdens that would shift to our protected communications would be extremely high. And I haven't done the operations research to prove this, but my suspicion is that if we lose unprotected communications, the protected satellites that we have do not have the throughput to be able to sustain the kind of data requirements that would be necessary for success in conventional operations.

So those would be at least two areas that I would focus on right away when one thinks about the vulnerability of our systems.

Mr. FORBES. Dr. Butterworth, if you could briefly tell us what you think the assessment would be of how it would impact our capabilities.

Dr. BUTTERWORTH. If I can figure out the button. There, I think that did it. Good. Thanks so much.

Mr. Chairman, it is a bit difficult to answer. It is easy enough to point to specific vulnerabilities and to try to identify the consequences of the loss of particular satellites or satellite functions. But I think my view on this is that we need to have a broader perspective and try to understand how space support is integrated into the joint fight. We haven't done a very good job of that.

We have tended to assume that there would be things from the space that would simply be available. I remember when I was running a project for General Cartwright years ago on foreign counterspace and so on, we would look at the annexes in PACOM [Pacific Command], for example, and the annex for space for their war plans was, "We assume space works." Now, it is not that way anyway; there is a much, much bigger annex these days. But that is the kind of approach that I think still exists throughout our work on this problem. So I would urge that we try to understand the integrated effect of fighting and not having the space systems and also alternative ways to get around it.

Second, just very briefly, we need to know an awful lot more not just about what is up there but what happens to our stuff. That can take a very long time. And I assume you will be digging into that in a subsequent hearing.

And then, finally, we need to integrate all the different command and control communications functions that Ashley, among others, was just talking about.

Mr. FORBES. Mr. Krepon.

Mr. KREPON. Mr. Chairman, in my view, the greatest current vulnerability is a debris vulnerability.

So, in 1985, the United States carried out a kinetic-energy ASAT test. Fourteen years later, a piece of debris from that test came within 1 mile of the newly launched International Space Station.

The debris problem has been magnified by some very, very large number, particularly after the Chinese ASAT test, but not just that ASAT test. There have been breakups of rocket bodies; there have been collisions. The debris problem is enormous. And we move the Space Station, on average, once a year to try and get out of the way of a piece of debris.

So the more a nation depends on space, the more vulnerable it becomes, just because of the debris problem—not even talking about Chinese counterspace capabilities.

Mr. FORBES. Okay. Thank you.

Mr. Rogers.

Mr. ROGERS. Thank you, Mr. Chairman.

Warning satellites do a great job of helping us to keep an eye on enemies for not only our national security but our allies'. I wondered, though, do you believe—is it your opinion that we have been clear to our adversaries on the risk they would incur by interfering with those satellites?

And I would start with you, Dr. Tellis.

Dr. TELLIS. I think we have tried to address the problem through indirection.

Mr. ROGERS. We haven't been direct enough?

Dr. TELLIS. I believe that is the case.

Mr. ROGERS. How about you, Dr. Butterworth?

Dr. BUTTERWORTH. Well, we have—as you well understand, Chairman, we have a problem that we don't want to be——

Mr. FORBES. Dr. Butterworth, hit that little button again. I know it is——

Dr. BUTTERWORTH. Thank you very much. I need to be trained frequently.

It is a difficult problem, as I know you gentlemen understand, that we don't want to be pointing out specific targets and specific vulnerabilities. So I agree that, yes, we have been sort of general in saying, ''Right, space is an important part of our military capabilities,'' without being terribly precise.

Mr. ROGERS. But do you think that we have explained to them there are consequences for messing with our satellites?

Dr. BUTTERWORTH. Sir, there is no doubt in my mind that they understand that very well——

Mr. ROGERS. Okay.

Dr. BUTTERWORTH [continuing]. That if they do something to our satellites, that means war. And I can't imagine why they would do something to a satellite if they weren't——

Mr. ROGERS. Mr. Krepon.

Mr. KREPON. Mr. Chairman, both President George W. Bush and President Obama have the same declaratory policy with respect to attacks on our space assets. I think declaratory policy—if you mess with our satellites, you are messing with our vital national security interests—that is an important piece. We have got that piece.

Mr. ROGERS. Do you think we have been clear on that?

Mr. KREPON. I think declaratory policy can't be a one-off. It needs to be repeated.

Mr. ROGERS. Well, let me ask this: Do you all believe that if our satellites were interfered with, that we have the capability to rapidly discern that and attribute who is disturbing the satellites?

Mr. KREPON. Proper retribution depends on attribution. And there are issues with respect to attribution.

Mr. ROGERS. Explain.

Mr. KREPON. Inferences could be drawn, but one of the reasons why I mentioned funding for space situational awareness to you is that that will help with attribution.

There are two kinds of challengers to us in space: One are actually little guys, and one are major powers. And, actually, most of the interference so far has been from the little guys, and the interference that they are most interested in is interfering with broadcast satellites.

Mr. ROGERS. Right.

Mr. KREPON. So our planning and strategies to respond, I think, depends on the category of adversary. But it all begins with attribution.

Mr. ROGERS. All right.

Dr. Butterworth or Dr. Tellis, do either of you think that we are short in our ability to attribute interference? Or do you think we are covered on that?

Dr. BUTTERWORTH. Sir, I think we are not just short, I think we are absent. Even if you are just talking about interference with communications satellites or something, it can take weeks and weeks and weeks to try to find out where that is coming from and then to try to find out who is actually doing it.

I urge the committee in different sessions to ask people, you know, how long would it take us to know that something had happened to one of our satellites.

Dr. TELLIS. I would make two points on that.

It depends on the kind of interference, and it depends on the context. There is some kind of interference that is palpable and manifest which is easier to attribute, and there are other kinds of interference, particularly electronic interference, that are harder to nail down. So that is point number one.

Point number two is, if the interference occurs in peacetime, where everything else is as is, it might be easier to attribute. But if it occurs in the context of a crisis or in war, when other systems are stressed greatly, I think the point that Dr. Butterworth made about the difficulties of attribution will only get magnified.

And, unfortunately, that is when attribution matters most. It is when other systems are stressed and it has a direct impact on your capability to prosecute military operations that we might pay the highest costs in our inability to attribute quickly.

Mr. FORBES. Mr. McIntyre.

Mr. MCINTYRE. Thank you very much.

Dr. Tellis, on page 2 of your testimony, you say that one of the concerns is China has steadily expanded its capability to mount discrete physical attacks on installations integral to the space-ground segment.

What is an example of that, how you could have a discrete physical attack on a ground segment?

Dr. TELLIS. By "discrete," I meant individual attacks as opposed to all-out attacks. And a specific example would be China's increasingly precise ballistic missile force that allows them to actually target sites as small as individual buildings at great distance without using the total force to achieve those effects.

Mr. MCINTYRE. Okay. Thank you. Thank you for clarifying that.

Dr. Butterworth, the last several years, we have seen China develop the ability to shoot down a satellite, perform new types of satellite maneuvers, and get closer to launching a new heavy-lift rocket.

When you look at this, what do you believe are the risks, when we talk about layering, as has been explained by Mr. Krepon, if we continue to rely on our legacy systems? Because I think the problem we have got here is our budget issues and knowing what to do, and unfortunately we know that too often military space programs are targeted for cuts.

And so the question is, how much can we rely on legacy programs and how much is new development that we need to do in order to provide the kind of multilayered protection that we would need?

Dr. BUTTERWORTH. Sir, I don't know any happy answer to that. It is going to take just a hell of a lot of money. We are going to have to start considering space as part of the joint fight, as part of the theater of operations, and that is going to require new systems.

I can't think of another way out of it. There is no silver bullet, there is no one thing that we can do, there is no specially orbiting laser, X-ray, nuclear pump device that will provide the defenses that we need. We are going to have to take it from design as part of the joint operating forces.

Is that responsive to your question?

Mr. MCINTYRE. That helps.

I don't know, since you used the term "multilayered defense," Mr. Krepon, if you would like to respond to that.

Mr. KREPON. The Stimson Center, where I work, put out a publication on how to tackle this problem of vulnerability and deterrence. And we had people writing from different points of view; we don't agree on some things. But every single one of these multilayered pieces we all agreed on.

Now, the diplomacy piece is the most contentious, and I know that many of you have your doubts. But I disagree with Bob about whether China is clear about the consequences of messing with our satellites.

We came to this understanding with Moscow during the cold war, but there was a whole lot more conversation between Washington and Moscow on strategic issues and space and nuclear than there is today between Washington and Beijing. So I am in favor of the diplomacy piece, too.

Mr. MCINTYRE. What do you believe is the nearest-term challenge with regard to our counterdefensive capability?

Mr. KREPON. You know, there are some vulnerabilities that we just can't escape, Mr. McIntyre. We can compensate for vulnerability as best we can, as budgets allow, but the vulnerability will continue to be there in space, and we can't talk ourselves out of that reality.

Satellites are immensely important, but they can be found, and major powers have the capability to mess with them. We certainly do have the capability to mess with the satellites of adversaries. They have it for us.

So how do we manage vulnerability as best we can? That is my view. That is the question.

Mr. MCINTYRE. Yeah. Thank you.

Thank you, Mr. Chairman.

Mr. FORBES. Mr. Cooper.

Mr. COOPER. Thank you, Mr. Chairman.

Mr. Krepon, I think it bears repeating that you said pretty directly that we had more communication during the cold war between America and the Soviet Union than we have today between America and China regarding space issues. That is a pretty startling realization. And that doesn't necessarily mean diplomacy, but communication, because there are many ways that information can be given back and forth.

So that would seem to be a startling risk factor in terms of both nations trying to behave in a rational fashion. Because the theory of mutually assured deterrence and the theory of most deterrence is that both actors understand each other's motivations. So I would think that would be an area for clarification.

Mr. KREPON. One of the problems we had with the Soviet Union early on was that the military had an outsized stake on national security issues. And I remember—I am showing my age, but when the strategic arms limitation talks began and our diplomats started talking about Soviet strategic forces, the military pulled our diplomats aside and said, you know, our diplomats are not cleared to hear this. Well, we got through that.

I think there is also dysfunction in China between the political leadership and the military. I don't see them meshing as well as I would like, particularly with respect to space.

So I think one of the potential gains in having more conversations is having military and civil leaders in China sitting down with our folks to talk about what our red lines are.

Mr. COOPER. Mr. Krepon, from a historical perspective, it is kind of amazing that—you know, Sputnik was such a long time ago; it is almost amazing that these other nations have taken so long to even begin to catch up. Because it has been many decades.

And these are high-class problems in the military sense, in the sense that you are not talking about civilian casualties, necessarily, here if a space asset is hit by debris or—you know, these are replaceable gizmos.

And, also, our military budget is completely within our discretion. And we represent a country with a per capita income of, what, $48,000 a person versus China with a per capita income of, what, $1,000 a person. And we are worried about maintaining our technological edge? You know, there shouldn't be that much of a concern if we want to do it. It is a question of will, not of means.

Mr. KREPON. Mr. Cooper, our capabilities to mess with somebody else's satellites have never been greater. And, unlike nuclear deterrence, we don't really need to be in your face about it. So we don't test new devices, we don't flight-test ASAT missiles, we don't deploy at high levels of readiness the way we do, or did, on the nuclear.

So the deterrence in space is largely inferred; it is not demonstrated in the same way. I think we still are able to get our points across with this latent or inferred capability: If you mess with us, the consequences could be immense, and they are of our choosing.

Mr. COOPER. Thank you, Mr. Chairman.

Mr. FORBES. Thank you.

The gentleman from Texas, Mr. Conaway, is recognized for 3 minutes.

Mr. CONAWAY. Thank you, Mr. Chair.

Thank you, gentlemen, for coming.

Mr. Krepon, you piqued my interest when you talked about, we need rules for space. Most rule-based systems—and I am a CPA [certified public accountant] by profession—are only as good as the enforcement process. Who would enforce those rules against the Chinese?

Mr. KREPON. Sir, we have rules of the road with respect to our navies, air forces, and ground forces operating in close proximity with Russia. These agreements exist. They do not have enforcement mechanisms. The nuclear arms reduction treaties that we have do not have enforcement mechanisms. The Non-Proliferation Treaty comes closest through concerted efforts at sanctions.

But we are talking not only about a rules-based system but a self-interested-based system, a national-interested-based system. So we——

Mr. CONAWAY. But don't we wind up just—I hear that and understand it. But some would argue that we have deluded ourselves in a lot of areas thinking bad guys or folks on the other side are as honest as we are, or we try to be. And so I hear that.

All three of you talked about hardening our existing fleet of satellites. What timeframe is that? How many years are you talking about, actually getting that accomplished?

Mr. KREPON. Sir, if you are talking about weight, weight gain for satellites, that is a very hard thing. So we tend to——

Mr. CONAWAY. Or protecting whatever you are trying to do to put self-defense mechanisms on them. You can't do those in space. This is a replace-the-entire-fleet issue, right?

Mr. KREPON. I think, given the sunk costs, we are thinking about, or I think about incremental——

Mr. CONAWAY. Okay.

Mr. KREPON [continuing]. Gains over time.

Mr. CONAWAY. Which orbits are most at risk? Every satellite up there, or just the ones in low Earth orbit?

Dr. BUTTERWORTH. Sir, I think the Chinese have recently demonstrated a high-altitude, direct-ascent ASAT capable of reaching GEO [geostationary orbit]. And they have certainly demonstrated the ability to be able to launch and deploy small items of considerable interest that are very difficult to track, and they can do that at a variety of altitudes, as well.

Mr. CONAWAY. Okay.

Thank you all. I appreciate your comments this afternoon.

I yield back.

Mr. FORBES. Mr. Langevin is recognized for 3 minutes.

Mr. LANGEVIN. Thank you, Mr. Chairman.

I want to thank our witnesses for being here today. I appreciate your testimony. I think it is a very important discussion.

Obviously, ensuring information dominance provided by our satellites is a difficult but absolutely critical topic. And I certainly, again, appreciate the committee's focus on this issue.

So I would like to—I would note that, given the proliferation of certain capabilities, this conversation certainly has relevance far beyond China. But I would like to focus on, for a minute, non-kinetic weapons, particularly high-energy lasers. Obviously, such weapons come with a variety of effects on a platform as complex as a satellite.

And what I want to know is, do we currently have the breadth of knowledge to characterize the full range of those effects across the spectrum of possible power levels and beam qualities?

Dr. BUTTERWORTH. I do not believe that we do have that information at present, sir.

We did some very small experiments a while ago, in the nineties, with the MSTI 5 satellite, and we cooked it as it came over New Mexico, I think it was, out of the Albuquerque range and were able to see how some of those effects were measured and what they might be.

But in terms of being able to really characterize the impact on us, I don't think so. I think we are still at the stage of putting warnings on the satellites that they are being lased, but I am not quite sure that we see clearly the effects.

Mr. LANGEVIN. Okay.

Anybody else care to comment?

Okay. Well, given the well-known vulnerabilities of satellites, the number of technologies that are able to threaten these platforms, is there an understood tiering of importance? For example, is there a particular importance attached to jamming or dazzling particular satellites?

Dr. TELLIS. There seems to be a trend, at least in the Chinese literature after 2007, after the 2007 test, that China ought to look at means other than simply kinetic attacks. Because I think one of the things that both shocked and surprised them was the international revulsion about the debris problem that was magnified as a result of that test.

And so certainly in recent years there has been a clear, I don't want to say a ''shift,'' but there has been an increase in the emphasis that China has placed essentially on soft kills or mission kills. Because it allows them to achieve their operational aims without contributing to destruction, physical destruction, of satellites, which obviously magnifies the debris problem, which affects them, as well.

Mr. LANGEVIN. And before my time runs out, how dependent is China's military and economically on U.S. systems such as GPS? And how long can we expect that dependence to persist, given current levels of investment in systems such as Beidou, if I am pronouncing that right?

Dr. BUTTERWORTH. I think Beidou is just about to finish up.

Isn't that right, Dr. Tellis?

Yeah. So it should be just complete.

What I suspect the Chinese are going to find, however, is that its performance is not up to that of the GPS system. And so they will very likely like to depend on the GPS system as long as possible, as well as using Beidou and trying to sell its appeal.

Mr. LANGEVIN. Okay.

Thank you, Mr. Chairman. Yield back.

Mr. FORBES. Mr. Byrne is recognized for 5 minutes.

Mr. BYRNE. Thank you.

I have one question, really following up on Mr. Cooper's question. And I am new, so this may be something that is so elementary that you are going to have to answer a very elementary question.

But you hear about the wealth or the productivity of China being so much less than the United States per capita and that they are spending so much less than we are on national defense. How in the world are they matching us in space in this sort of technology? Are they focusing a disproportionate share of their resources on that? Are we not focusing enough of our resources on it? How could a country like that come close to the United States of America?

Mr. KREPON. For an elementary question, it is a very difficult one.

It drives me nuts to read the trade literature about how much we put into space. And I think we are shortchanging space across the board, in my view.

Bear in mind that it has taken China four decades to catch up with us in terms of—and they haven't caught up with us yet—in terms of space exploration. They are still behind us, in my judgment, across the board.

But they are working hard, and they are taking shortcuts. So is this worrisome? In my view, it is. And resources can't solve the problem, but I don't think you can begin to solve the problem without more resources on our end.

Mr. BYRNE. I know I have just a little bit of time. I just want to make sure I get down to this. What should we be doing that we are not doing to stay significantly ahead of the Chinese?

Mr. KREPON. Here I am going to provoke Ashley and Bob.

I think that on the counterspace side, I think we are doing a fair amount. The thing that sticks in my craw has to do more with the exploration piece. And, you know, it would be—we are having trouble building satellites on time and on budget. We are getting a little bit better, but we are handicapping ourselves so much by the way we do things, our procurement policies. We are just not on time, on budget.

Dr. TELLIS. Could I take a crack at answering that in a direct way?

I think we have two weaknesses. Our space systems are too concentrated in their capability and they are too few, which means that any loss of even a single system has a disproportionate effect on our capacity.

We have done this for both technological and economic reasons. If you move to an alternative architecture of smaller satellites, more flexible, more distributed capabilities, it is going to be more costly, but the upside is that we will have greater resilience and greater ability to compensate for losses.

The second weakness that we have is that we have a very poor reconstitution capacity. If we lose some of these space systems in a war, it is going to take a long time before we can get replacements up there. And that is everything from a lack of spares, in terms of the space systems themselves, all the way to a long timeline with respect to launch.

So we have simply not configured our capacities on the principle that these assets are at risk. And that is the point I think that Dr. Butterworth was making, that we have simply been content to assume that we will have these capabilities no matter what.

If we begin to shift that premise and think about these capabilities as essentially nonavailable in some circumstances, I think we would begin to think of our investments in space in a very different way.

Mr. FORBES. The gentleman's time has expired.

And we saved the clean-up spot for the distinguished gentleman from the great State of Mississippi, Mr. Palazzo.

Mr. PALAZZO. Thank you, Mr. Chairman.

Space situational awareness is an issue that influences every space asset beyond those of national security space. The animation showing the creation of debris from the 2007 China ASAT test or the 2009 Iridium-Cosmos collision are dramatic depictions of the consequence of the laws of motion in our space environment.

I suspect most people in the room today are familiar with the recent hit movie ''Gravity.'' I think the movie did everyone here a service by bringing to light the reality of the precarious situation of space operations in our orbitable environment. It is obvious that the consequences of a conflict in space could be devastating to nearly all space-faring nations.

So, with that, I would like to get the witnesses' thoughts on the priority of space situational awareness [SSA] for U.S. space security. And, also, is the United States Air Force Space Command the proper entity into which we should expand a greater SSA responsibility? And if not the Space Command, then who?

And we will start with Dr. Tellis.

Dr. TELLIS. I think space situational awareness is the foundation for any kind of defensive counterspace that the U.S. has to invest in.

I accept the point that Mr. Krepon made in principle, that we don't need to overinvest in offensive counterspace because we have latent capabilities to do that if required under conditions of extremis.

But if we have to do serious defensive counterspace, the challenge of being able to attribute where the threats are coming from, what the nature of the threat is all takes on an entirely different coloration. And we certainly have to put resources first and foremost into space situational awareness, because nothing else with respect to defensive counterspace is going to work if you don't have adequate situational awareness. So that is point number one.

Point number two, I think my view is that Air Force Space Command is the logical place in which this should reside because the Air Force maintains the largest catalogue of space objects out there. It has the resources, both terrestrial and space-borne, to maintain this capability. And I think starting from scratch or moving it to a different organization at this point would involve probably more trouble than it is worth.

Mr. PALAZZO. Dr. Butterworth.

Dr. BUTTERWORTH. Yes, sir, I would concur with what Dr. Tellis was saying, with a couple of qualifications.

One is that I think we should emphasize space situational awareness from orbit. And some of those orbits should be very high so that we are looking down. There may be an effort to try to make things difficult to detect. Nothing is equally difficult to detect from all angles. We should have all angles from which we could survey what is out there in space.

Secondly, with regard to the Air Force's capabilities, I would note that the record of the JMS [JSpOC Mission System] out there, or the JSpOC [Joint Space Operations Center], is not overwhelmingly impressive. And so I hope we can do a lot better with that soon.

Mr. PALAZZO. Thank you.

Mr. KREPON. Sir, I would like to put a bug in your ear about space traffic management, because situational awareness goes hand-in-hand with traffic management. One of the reasons why we want situational awareness is to get early warning, but it is also to avoid collisions with debris or, heck, another satellite.

So we haven't really thought hard about space traffic management. How do we do that? Who does it? How does it work? Capabilities are so disproportionate. We are the best. But how do we convey messages? How do we develop patterns of safe traffic in space? We are behind the eight ball on this one.

Mr. PALAZZO. Thank you.

Mr. FORBES. And, gentlemen, we once again thank you for being here.

I thank my good friend, Mike Rogers, for allowing us to join and have this joint hearing.

As I told you earlier today, we want to give you 60 seconds or so for any wrap-up that you have of something that you think you need to clarify or that we left out. Because it is not just important, this hearing, but it is important, the record we are building of this hearing, to be used later.

Dr. Tellis, if you don't mind, we will start back with you because you had the first opening remarks.

Dr. TELLIS. Thank you, Mr. Chairman.

I just want to make one point, which Mr. Krepon referred to, because I think it is important.

I am not as sanguine about the idea that we will have a collaborative solution or even an equilibrium solution with respect to counterspace where China is concerned in a way that we had with the Soviet Union during the cold war. And there is a very important reason for that, and it goes beyond diplomacy.

There was no asymmetric dependence on space at the height of the cold war. Both the Soviets and the United States, certainly in the latter half of the cold war, came to depend on space almost equally for the success of their military operations. And, therefore, Soviet incentives to engage in counterspace activities of the kind that the Chinese are contemplating were much smaller.

China's dependence on space is not as significant as the U.S. dependence on space. And it is that delta independence that gives China much greater freedom of action than we recognize. It is something to keep in mind.

There is a second point. During the old cold war days, the Soviets had the conventional advantage. And, therefore, if conflict broke out, they could have been content prosecuting their operational aims through the use of conventional forces alone because that was their strong suit.

The Chinese see themselves as not having that kind of a conventional advantage. And, therefore, the incentives they have to attack us asymmetrically, to attack our space assets, to attack our information architecture, and so on and so forth is much greater.

And so I think we need to be sensitive to the differences that exist in the U.S.-China case compared to the U.S.-Soviet case, which makes the burden on the objective of protecting our space assets even more.

Thank you.

Mr. FORBES. Thank you, Dr. Tellis.

Dr. Butterworth.

Dr. BUTTERWORTH. Thank you, Chairman. And thank you again for having this excellent hearing.

I will endorse almost everything that my colleague to my right here said, except for the part about the Soviet Union. Even they didn't use space in the way that we have. Nobody does it like we do. We showed the world first in Desert Storm the integration of space assets into tactical operations, and we have gone way beyond what we could do then in the ensuing 25 years, or almost 25 years.

Nobody else has tried to do that. They may use it for strategic reconnaissance, they may use it for selected communications, and so on, but not integrated into warfare the way that we have.

And so, to try to understand the relationship with China in terms of parallelism or symmetry—that is, you know, that we can shoot their satellites and they can shoot ours—misses the point that they don't use space in the way that we do, nor, as I mentioned, did the Soviet Union.

And so when I talk about trying to take into account the joint fight perspective, that is the most important part of it, is to understand that they are looking at space with very different eyes, just as Dr. Tellis was just suggesting.

18

Thank you again.

Mr. FORBES. Thank you, Dr. Butterworth.

Dr. Krepon.

Mr. KREPON. Mr. Chairman, China's vulnerability in space is growing every year—every year. And the question that you are exploring here, for which I thank you, is, how do we leverage this to influence Beijing's national calculus? And I don't feel comfortable that we understand Beijing's national calculus enough. So I would like more conversations, U.S.-China, on this.

Mr. FORBES. Okay.

Gentlemen, thank you all.

Thank all of our Members for being here.

Mr. Rogers, thank you.

And, with that, we are adjourned.

[Whereupon, at 4:30 p.m., the subcommittees were adjourned.]

APPENDIX

JANUARY 28, 2014

PREPARED STATEMENTS SUBMITTED FOR THE RECORD

JANUARY 28, 2014

**Opening Remarks of the Honorable J. Randy Forbes for the
Seapower and Projection Forces and Strategic Forces Subcommittee
Joint Hearing on the People's Republic of China's Counterspace Program
and the Implications for U.S. National Security
January 28, 2014**

Welcome to the joint Seapower and Projection Forces Subcommittee and Strategic Forces Subcommittee hearing on the counterspace program of the People's Republic of China and the implications for U.S. National Security. This hearing is part of our ongoing, bipartisan Asia-Pacific Oversight Series. I want to thank my good friend, Chairman Rogers of the Subcommittee on Strategic Forces, for working with me on this important area.

Our two subcommittees are concerned with developments that could pose threats to U.S. space systems, and this hearing is intended as an open, unclassified dialogue regarding these threats, the damage they could do to U.S. space systems, and the options for mitigating these threats. I believe this Nation's national security policy benefits when we can have an open and frank conversation that assesses the merits of our current trajectory and direction.

In recent years, we have become increasingly aware of our dependence on our space systems and of other countries pursuing technology that could hold our critical national security space systems at risk. Allow me to mention two examples that highlight this point.

In 2007, the People's Republic of China destroyed one of their own weather satellites in a test of an anti-satellite weapon, by launching a missile armed with a kinetic kill vehicle. This weather satellite was around 500 miles above Earth in low Earth orbit. While not known at the time, this ASAT test was a wake-up call for China watchers in our government who continued to believe that China had a long way to go before developing anti-access technologies to challenge U.S. military dominance in the Western Pacific.

And more recently, we've learned from the U.S. – China Economic and Security Review Commission's 2013 Report to Congress that, on May 13th of 2013, China launched a missile that went to a very high-altitude into space. No satellite was put in orbit for this test, and the recent report to Congress noted that, and I quote, "available data suggest[s] it was intended to test at least the launch vehicle component of a new high-altitude anti-satellite (or A-SAT) capability."

I am very concerned about the implications associated with China's development of anti-satellite capabilities. The scholar Tom Christenson remarked over a decade ago that China could "pose (military) problems without catching up" by investing in asymmetric capabilities that undermine America's traditional military advantages. Space is one of these primary areas that the United States uses to leverage its global power-projection and we now see China seeking to threaten this domain as part of its "counter-intervention" strategy. It is a clear national security interest to ensure that the United States retains freedom of action in the space warfare domain.

To help us better understand this situation, we have three distinguished witnesses here today.

Our witnesses are:

Dr. Ashley J. Tellis
Senior Associate
Carnegie Endowment for International Peace

Dr. Robert L. Butterworth
President
Aries Analytics, Inc

And,

Mr. Michael Krepon
Co-Founder
Stimson Center

I want to express our appreciation to our witnesses in advance for their preparation and for taking time out of their busy schedules to help us understand this subject more completely.

I'm going to first turn to my colleague, Chairman Rogers, for his opening statement.

Opening Remarks – <u>As Prepared for Delivery</u>

The Honorable Michael D. Rogers
Chairman, Subcommittee on Strategic Forces
House Armed Services Committee

Hearing on "People's Republic of China's Counterspace Program and the
Implications for U.S. National Security"

January 28, 2014

Thank you Chairman Forbes. I greatly appreciate your leadership of the oversight activities the committee has been conducting in regards to the Administration's "pivot to the Asia-Pacific".

For quite a while, we had the benefit of enjoying space as a sanctuary. That time is over. As has been said before, space is congested, contested and competitive. We must therefore focus on how we will defend our freedom of action in space and we must be crystal clear with our adversaries about the consequences for taking us on in space. One thing is clear, our adversaries are developing an arsenal of weapons to disrupt and destroy our satellites, and we need to have the full range of capabilities to defend ourselves and our allies from any aggression.

I would also like to welcome our witnesses, and express my appreciation for their support of this important hearing. Thank you.

The People's Republic of China's Counterspace Program and the Implications for U.S. National Security

Opening Statement for Ranking Member Mike McIntyre
January 28, 2014

- Today's joint hearing will focus on recent developments by the People's Republic of China in counterspace capabilities and their potential implications for U.S. National Security.

- I want to thank Strategic Forces Subcommittee Chairman Mike Rogers and Ranking Member Jim Cooper for working with me and Chairman Forbes to make this a joint hearing.

- Over the last several years, we have seen China's abilities in space gather steam – from the 2007 kinetic hit on its weather satellite to recent developments in its ability to maneuver satellites, to its long-term effort to increase its long-range launch capabilities.

- Today I'd like to hear from our witnesses their views on China's recent counterspace activities and their views on what the U.S. should focus on to strengthen its deterrent options.

- To begin, what specifically are the threats? What technologies and strategies should we be focused on to bolster our counterspace defenses?

- For example, how effective would it be to disaggregate our satellite capabilities? Or are there other approaches that might be more effective?

- Then, I'd like to discuss potential options if deterrence does not work. For example, if there were a scenario where China disabled one of our space assets, what would be an appropriate response?

- And in a worst-case scenario, what should we be doing to ensure we could still operate and defend our national interests if we ever found ourselves in a completely denied space environment?

- To be clear, China's motives in space are not yet clear, and it is not the intent of this hearing to make assumptions.

- However it is clear to me that China and the United States are in a growing competition for access to space and control of space.

- And it is the responsibility of this committee to consider all possibilities, including that China's improved capabilities may one day degrade the United States' ability to securely operate in space.

- Taking a hard look at all possibilities helps us make better budget decisions to ensure our space assets are appropriately protected, resourced and connected.

With that, thank you for taking the time to be with us today and I look forward to your comments.

CARNEGIE
ENDOWMENT FOR
INTERNATIONAL PEACE

Congressional Testimony

CHINA'S COUNTERSPACE PROGRAMS—ONLY MORE BAD NEWS

Testimony by **Dr. Ashley J. Tellis**
Senior Associate, South Asia Program
Carnegie Endowment for International Peace

House Armed Services Subcommittee on
Strategic Forces and the Subcommittee on
Seapower and Projection Forces
January 28, 2014

Good afternoon, Chairman Rogers, Chairman Forbes, distinguished Ranking Members, and Members of the Subcommittees. Thank you for your kind invitation to testify on China's counterspace programs and their impact on the United States. I respectfully request that my statement be entered into the record.

In my view, the current and evolving Chinese counterspace threat to U.S. military operations in the Asia-Pacific theater ranks on par with the dangers posed by Chinese offensive cyber operations to the United States. The dangers emanating from China's counterspace investments are real and growing. And the diversity of Chinese counterspace activities ensures that almost every U.S. space component—the space systems in orbit, the links that control them and channel their data, and their associated ground facilities—will face grave perils as current Chinese counterspace programs mature and their technologies are integrated into the People's Liberation Army's (PLA) warfighting arsenal. The need for compensating U.S. investments to defeat these emerging threats is, therefore, vital if the extant U.S. military superiority that is essential to protecting the United States, its allies, and its interests is to be safeguarded.

The international community still vividly remembers the events of January 11, 2007, when a Chinese SC-19 direct-ascent anti-satellite (ASAT) weapon destroyed an aging Chinese weather satellite in low Earth orbit (LEO) through a successful hit-to-kill intercept. That test evoked considerable revulsion because the near doubling of space debris it produced threatens all space platforms, including China's own. A little over six years later, on May 13, 2013, China conducted yet another test—after several other experiments in the intervening years—of what is almost certainly a new direct-ascent ASAT system. This test, which the U.S. Department of Defense laconically described as a missile launch "on a ballistic trajectory to nearly geosynchronous Earth orbit" (GEO), however, did not receive the international attention that followed the January 2007 event.

Yet it should nevertheless be disconcerting to U.S. defense planners because it further corroborates China's continuing intention to develop and maintain the capacity to kinetically target U.S. space systems that are positioned even in high Earth orbits. If the January 2007 test proved that China can range critical U.S. space systems in low Earth orbit, such as meteorological and electro-optical surveillance satellites, the May 2013 test indicates that vital U.S. space systems even in higher orbits, such as precision navigation and timing, infrared surveillance, and advanced communications satellites, are now vulnerable to the threat of direct-ascent kinetic attacks by China.

In the aftermath of the January 2007 ASAT test, I had argued that China's counterspace program—of which the direct-ascent ASAT weapon was only one component among many—was "part of a considered strategy designed to counter the overall military capability of the United States" (Ashley J. Tellis, "China's Military Space Strategy," *Survival*, Vol. 49, No. 3/Autumn 2007). Nothing has occurred in the Chinese counterspace program since that time to compel a revision of that judgment. In fact, the evolving developments in the program since that 2007 event only suggest that many of the alternative explanations that were adduced then for China's counterspace activities have proven unsustainable.

The idea that the Chinese direct-ascent ASAT weapon program is evidence more of "technological determinism" or bureaucratic politics than part of a studied menu of counterspace options is hard to fathom given the immensity, diversity, and focus of the myriad efforts involved. This contention was unreal in 2007 and it is even more so today, when Chinese counterspace activities have expanded both in their range and scale. Thus, for example, in recent years, China has steadily expanded its:

- space-object surveillance and identification systems (SOSI) through new advanced optical and radar systems
- direct-ascent and co-orbital ASAT programs to include new kinetic systems as well as exotic devices such as robotic arms that can be used to disturb or disrupt satellite orbits
- activities involving high- and low-energy lasers and high-powered microwave weapon systems
- electronic warfare acquisitions involving a diverse set of jammers intended to paralyze U.S. satellite communications systems in both military and civilian bands
- computer network attack capabilities which are increasingly intended to target, among other things, both space systems and their ground networks
- capability to mount discrete physical attacks on installations integral to the space ground segment

Moreover, all these programs only complement China's longstanding ability to execute a "Samson option" involving the detonation of nuclear weapons in space.

Whether assessed individually or in their totality, these endeavors remain initiatives of strategic significance that are authorized ultimately by the Central Military Commission (CMC). There is no evidence which suggests that these programs are the products of "freelancing" by the various research institutions and industrial conglomerates involved in the development and production of counterspace systems. To the contrary, China's counterspace activities are principally directed by the PLA's General Armaments Department and to a lesser degree by the General Staff Department, although the latter remains the nodal body that directs the subordinate services that have physical custody of the various counterspace components in wartime. This system of centralized control suggests that a high degree of deliberation drives the entire chain of Chinese counterspace activities to include the programmatic definition of requirements, research and development, acquisition of the various systems and their subsequent integration into the combat arms, all the way to operational deployment in the field in preparation for final employment when directed.

The idea that Chinese counterspace activities would diminish in intensity as Beijing slowly became a space power of significance has also proven to be illusory. Without a doubt, China is a major spacefaring nation today. The number of annual Chinese space launches currently exceeds that of the United States and it is believed that China presently operates some 105 satellites in space, just six short of the number required to surpass the Russian satellite inventory in orbit right now. Chinese satellites today span the gamut from weather and navigation platforms to communications and remote sensing, from electro-optical surveillance and synthetic aperture radar systems to electronic intelligence collection platforms. The Chinese space program more generally is attempting to push the boundaries of innovation with its manned spaceflight and lunar exploration components as well as through other development activities such as its spaceplane and hypersonic glide vehicle programs.

Even as China has expanded these investments in space, however, its commitment to developing a wide range of counterspace capabilities—targeted principally at the United States but also applicable to other spacefaring powers—has not diminished. This antinomous dynamic is driven by two realities. First, even as China seeks to use space for its own national goals, it is determined to develop and employ counterspace technologies whenever necessary to neutralize the combat advantages enjoyed by its opponents in the event of a conflict, while at the same time utilizing these burgeoning capabilities to deter any adversary attacks on its own space systems. Second, although the goals of Chinese counterspace employment vis-à-vis a superior adversary, such as the United States, may subsist in tension with China's own professed desire for a peaceful space environment, Beijing appears to have concluded that the "delta" between its own and Washington's dependence on space for the fulfillment of their respective national aims favors China rather than the United States. In other words, although competing counterspace actions by both nations would be hazardous to their common interests, the United States would stand to lose more than China does, given the relatively greater American dependence on space for both civilian and military purposes. Based on such an assessment, prosecuting counterspace operations in a crisis may be rational for China in any significant Sino-U.S. conflict along its periphery, even though Beijing itself stands to lose considerably as a result of the expected American riposte.

Finally, the idea that China is deeply invested in its counterspace programs because the United States has proven resistant to space arms control is also fallacious. The Chinese interest in counterspace solutions has little to do with Washington's attitude to space arms control, although numerous Chinese commentators continue to advance this argument. Beijing's investments in counterspace capabilities, rather, are deeply rooted in the political predicaments it faces—none of which can be remedied by any arms control solutions. To begin with, China believes that it is engaged in a major geopolitical competition with the United States, a struggle wherein war, however remote, is still possible. Such a war could arise either because of extant disagreements, for example over Taiwan, which get out of hand; or because regional crises involving American protectees, such as Japan, explode to bring Chinese and American military power into confrontation; or because intensifying Sino-American competition in the Indo-Pacific spins out of control at some point during the next few decades when a power transition appears to be underway in Asia and possibly at the core of the international system.

Irrespective of what specific provocation may spark a wider conflict, Chinese defense planners are deeply consumed by the necessity of preparing for an armed confrontation with the United States, which they clearly recognize as a superior military power. Given their assessment that American superiority derives fundamentally from its ability to leverage its space systems to produce the information dominance necessary to deliver decisive warfighting advantages, Chinese strategists are by necessity drawn to the idea of attempting to neutralize American space capabilities. This lure becomes all the more tantalizing because not only is U.S. space superiority critical for the success of American military operations but its space architecture is as a rule remarkably vulnerable to offensive actions undertaken by an adversary.

This reality has driven Chinese counterspace programs ever since the United States was able to demonstrate the importance of information dominance during Operation Desert Storm and it continues to animate Chinese counterspace ambitions to this day. Because Chinese planners judge that their best chance to neutralize American information dominance hinges on undermining its space superiority, they are unlikely to restrain their counterspace programs, either unilaterally or through an arms control regime, until such time as they can satisfy their ambition to defeat American military power through means other than counterspace operations. Even as they continue to pursue such goals, however, China will continue to blame the United States for, as one Chinese military officer, Senior Colonel Zhao Dexi, put it, "maintain[ing] its absolute advantage in space even at the expense of other nations' security…[and]… promoting its policy on space control while vigorously developing its military force in space, including space weapons…[while]… oppos[ing] holding talks on [the] non-weaponization of outer space."

The Chinese critique about the supposed U.S. weaponization of outer space is indeed specious and is intended largely to deflect attention from the fact that China's principal counterspace capabilities are not routinely in space and will not traverse it until actually employed in wartime. It is in fact ironic that, thanks to China's diverse counterspace investments, Beijing is more likely to be the first to actually weaponize space—that is to introduce systems that serve as weapons in space—despite its insistent and avowed claims that "China is not engaged in any space arms race at present, nor will it be in the future" (Senior Colonel Zhao Dexi, "Challenges to Space Interests and Our Strategic Choices," *China Military Science*, March 2010, Open Source Center, CPP20100921563002, September 21, 2010).

Despite the wide variety of counterspace investments that China currently is pursuing, it is unclear whether Beijing seeks—as a matter of pre-established doctrine—to wrest space superiority through widespread kinetic attacks on U.S. space systems right from the very start of a conflict. Part of this uncertainty derives from the lack of information about whether the CMC has promulgated a formal counterspace doctrine, though it has been clear for some time now that the PLA has, utilizing U.S. and Russian approaches, already developed different components of such a doctrine which emphasize different dimensions of space control to include what in the United States is termed space situational awareness as well as defensive and offensive counterspace. Moreover, many of the constituent elements of these mission areas, as manifested in the Chinese counterspace repertoire, are already integrated into campaign planning at the operational level. Since the last decade, in any case, a large literature involving Chinese theorizing about space warfare operations has emerged and if the 2007 ASAT test appears to have taught Chinese space thinkers anything at all, it is that kinetic attacks on space systems produce dangerous amounts of debris that could be perilous to China's own space systems and space operations.

A significant number of Chinese space warfare theorists seem to have accordingly converged on the position that the capabilities to execute kinetic attacks on an adversary's space systems, along with the willingness to undertake such attacks, must be ever present for the success of deterrence—understood as preventing attacks on one's own space systems or preventing an escalation that involves attacks on one's own space systems. But the actual prosecution of such kinetic attacks should be utilized only when peacetime and crisis signaling fails or when dictated by the invincible operational necessities of war. Irrespective of when or how kinetic attacks are employed, however, most Chinese space warfare theorists conceive of their counterspace operations as contributing to the acquisition of space superiority. Because of China's current technological and space order-of-battle limitations, however, such superiority is understood not as encompassing dominance over all of outer space but rather as limited control that constrains the operations of an adversary's space and conventional warfighting capabilities sufficiently to enable the PLA's own units to achieve their specific operational objectives.

Given this conception of the role of counterspace instruments in military operations, Chinese theorists appear to be laying the foundations for justifying increased investments in capabilities aimed at the disruption of space operations—or, in other words, securing episodic effects—and the denial of space-derived information necessary for exercising conventional superiority in a given battlespace—or, in other words, securing persistent effects—over and above the preexisting investments made in developing kinetic kill systems, which can only contribute to the war effort by the destruction of an adversary's space assets either in orbit or on the ground. This quest for new counterspace capabilities that provide transient and reversible effects rather than simply permanent and irreversible destruction seems to have acquired renewed emphasis in Chinese theorizing after the 2007 ASAT test, and it appears driven by the need to avert unintended escalation and compel the adversary to terminate his aggression while simultaneously enabling Chinese conventional forces to secure their operational aims.

The prevalence of such theorizing suggests that China is moving towards a space campaign posture that emphasizes a variety of counterspace activities ranging from measured actions that produce transient and reversible effects ("soft-kills") to the extreme violence of kinetic attacks, which are best reserved only for the apex of escalation or when dictated by dire operational necessity. Such a concept of operations is obviously "better" than simply a kinetic war of all against all in space and on the ground, but at the end of the day it cannot be consoling to U.S. defense planners in any significant way. For starters, it is not clear whether these visions purveyed by Chinese space warfare theorists, no matter how thoughtful or well situated, represent the actual operational preferences of the planners or the warfighters in the Chinese military. Notions of graduated escalation have long been alien to Chinese military culture and its style of combat operations. But even if this represents the new inclinations of the PLA, the emphasis on counterspace operations that emphasize securing transient and reversible effects only imply that space will no longer be a protected sanctuary in the context of any future U.S.-China confrontation. Rather, it will be a heavily contested environment, where the U.S. military will have to struggle to secure the information dominance that it simply presumed in the past would automatically obtain, when all it had to do then was to employ that freely found dominance to produce conventional victories on the ground, at sea, and in the air.

The immensity of the burdens associated with securing this information dominance in an era when all U.S. intelligence, surveillance, and reconnaissance (ISR), communications, and other combat support systems will be under persistent attack—even if they are not physically destroyed—cannot be underestimated. Even if Beijing eschews kinetic attacks on U.S. space systems and their ground segments in the early phases of a Chinese counterspace campaign, U.S. military forces will have to apply enormous effort toward: defeating Chinese deception and denial operations; mitigating the Chinese jamming of all critical U.S. space systems to include the Global Positioning System constellation and its terrestrial receivers, space-based synthetic aperture radars, major satellite communication systems, and the links that ensure the effectiveness of the electro-optical and infrared surveillance systems; protecting all satellites from laser dazzling and damage; and, warding off cyber attacks on the space control networks and eventually against the space systems themselves. Thus, even if kinetic attacks against satellites and their ground segments by direct-ascent, co-orbital, nuclear and missile weapons, and special forces are excluded from consideration, the challenges confronting the U.S. military in regard to sustaining the information dominance it has traditionally enjoyed—in the face of current and prospective Chinese counterspace capabilities—will be enormous. Furthermore, given that kinetic counterspace attacks cannot be ruled out at any point in the event of a conflict, the U.S. military will have to simply prepare for all eventualities, irrespective of what Chinese space warfare theorists contend is either plausible or desirable.

The United States is eminently capable of dealing with the threats posed by Chinese counterspace investments through both defensive and offensive counterspace responses of its own, but these will necessarily require significant financial resources if they are to be successfully brought to fruition. Since I have outlined broadly the technical measures required in these areas in my article cited earlier—"China's Military Space Strategy"—I will not repeat them here. Suffice it to say that because protecting U.S. information dominance is vital not only to securing success in war but also to procuring that victory at the lowest cost in terms of lives and effort expended, both the administration and the Congress should not stint in funding all the mitigation efforts required to defeat China's counterspace initiatives—the term "defeat" in this context understood as enabling the U.S. military to successfully complete its missions despite opposition.

Let me end by offering a few concluding thoughts on the policy responses the United States should pursue in regards to responding to China's counterspace programs. Unfortunately for both the United States and the international community, there is no arms control solution available to limit the dangers posed by China's counterspace activities. There are already deep and abiding disagreements universally about what constitutes weaponization in space, which instruments ought to be considered space weapons, and whether and how U.S. space policies have contributed to space competition. All these controversies ensure that a useful space arms control regime capable of restraining counterspace activities by any state, including China, is very far away, if it is at all possible.

Given this fact, the United States must prepare to cope with China's counterspace programs principally through unilateral investments in developing the appropriate antidotes. It should initiate a discussion with all spacefaring powers about the nature of emerging threats to security in space and it should certainly engage in consultation with its friends and allies, especially in Asia—including Japan, South Korea, India, and Australia, among others—about the challenges posed by China's counterspace program. A conversation with China about space security too would be worthwhile, but it should not be assumed that such discussions, no matter how intense, will produce a convergence in perceptions. The United States should also continue to monitor the on-going discussions about the International Code of Conduct for Outer Space Activities supported by the European Union. But even if these deliberations ultimately produce a document that the United States finds worthwhile to sign on to, it bears remembering that neither the Code nor for that matter the proposed Treaty on Prevention of the Placement of Weapons in Outer Space and of the Threat or Use of Force Against Outer Space Objects (PPWT) actually address the problematic threats to space security posed by China's counterspace investments. Regrettably, therefore, the United States is condemned to manage this hazard mainly through its own resources because, given China's political objectives and strategic constraints, even good confidence-building measures are unlikely to constrain its evolving counterspace warfare programs in any meaningful way.

Ashley J. Tellis

EDUCATION

PhD, MA, University of Chicago
MA, BA, University of Bombay

Ashley J. Tellis is a senior associate at the Carnegie Endowment for International Peace specializing in international security, defense, and Asian strategic issues. While on assignment to the U.S. Department of State as senior adviser to the under secretary of state for political affairs, he was intimately involved in negotiating the civil nuclear agreement with India.

Previously, he was commissioned into the Foreign Service and served as senior adviser to the ambassador at the U.S. embassy in New Delhi. He also served on the National Security Council staff as special assistant to the president and senior director for strategic planning and Southwest Asia.

Prior to his government service, Tellis was senior policy analyst at the RAND Corporation and professor of policy analysis at the RAND Graduate School.

He is the author of *India's Emerging Nuclear Posture* (RAND, 2001) and co-author of *Interpreting China's Grand Strategy: Past, Present, and Future* (RAND, 2000). He is the research director of the Strategic Asia Program at the National Bureau of Asian Research and co-editor of the program's ten most recent annual volumes, including this year's *Strategic Asia 2013–14: Asia in the Second Nuclear Age*. In addition to numerous Carnegie and RAND reports, his academic publications have appeared in many edited volumes and journals, and he is frequently called to testify before Congress.

Tellis is a member of several professional organizations related to defense and international studies including the Council on Foreign Relations, the International Institute of Strategic Studies, the United States Naval Institute, and the Navy League of the United States.

DISCLOSURE FORM FOR WITNESSES
CONCERNING FEDERAL CONTRACT AND GRANT INFORMATION

INSTRUCTION TO WITNESSES: Rule 11, clause 2(g)(5), of the Rules of the U.S. House of Representatives for the 113th Congress requires nongovernmental witnesses appearing before House committees to include in their written statements a curriculum vitae and a disclosure of the amount and source of any federal contracts or grants (including subcontracts and subgrants) received during the current and two previous fiscal years either by the witness or by an entity represented by the witness. This form is intended to assist witnesses appearing before the House Committee on Armed Services in complying with the House rule. Please note that a copy of these statements, with appropriate redactions to protect the witness's personal privacy (including home address and phone number) will be made publicly available in electronic form not later than one day after the witness's appearance before the committee.

Witness name: __Ashley J. Tellis__

Capacity in which appearing: (check one)

_x_ Individual

____Representative

If appearing in a representative capacity, name of the company, association or other entity being represented:

FISCAL YEAR 2013

federal grant(s)/ contracts	federal agency	dollar value	subject(s) of contract or grant
	DOD	$68,000	Indian Ocean
	NIC	$12,250	NIC Associates

FISCAL YEAR 2012

federal grant(s)/ contracts	federal agency	dollar value	subject(s) of contract or grant
	DOD	$66,000	Indian Ocean
	NIC	$11,750	NIC Associates
	LLNL	$5,400	South Asia

FISCAL YEAR 2011

Federal grant(s) / contracts	federal agency	dollar value	subject(s) of contract or grant
	NIC	$8,000	NIC Associates

Federal Contract Information: If you or the entity you represent before the Committee on Armed Services has contracts (including subcontracts) with the federal government, please provide the following information:

Number of contracts (including subcontracts) with the federal government:

      Current fiscal year (2013):_2_____;
      Fiscal year 2012:_____3_____;
      Fiscal year 2011:_____1_____.

Federal agencies with which federal contracts are held:

      Current fiscal year (2013):__DOD, NIC_____;
      Fiscal year 2012:_____DOD, NIC, LLNL_____;
      Fiscal year 2011:_____NIC_____.

List of subjects of federal contract(s) (for example, ship construction, aircraft parts manufacturing, software design, force structure consultant, architecture & engineering services, etc.):

      Current fiscal year (2013):___Indian Ocean, NIC Associates_____;
      Fiscal year 2012:_____Indian Ocean, NIC Associates, South Asia____;
      Fiscal year 2011:_____NIC Associates_____.

Aggregate dollar value of federal contracts held:

      Current fiscal year (2013):___$80,250_____;
      Fiscal year 2012:_____$83,150_____;
      Fiscal year 2011:_____$8,000_____.

Federal Grant Information: If you or the entity you represent before the Committee on Armed Services has grants (including subgrants) with the federal government, please provide the following information:

Number of grants (including subgrants) with the federal government:

       Current fiscal year (2013):_____;
       Fiscal year 2012:_____;
       Fiscal year 2011:_____.

Federal agencies with which federal grants are held:

       Current fiscal year (2013):_____;
       Fiscal year 2012:_____;
       Fiscal year 2011:_____.

List of subjects of federal grants(s) (for example, materials research, sociological study, software design, etc.):

       Current fiscal year (2013):_____;
       Fiscal year 2012:_____;
       Fiscal year 2011:_____.

Aggregate dollar value of federal grants held:

       Current fiscal year (2013):_____;
       Fiscal year 2012:_____;
       Fiscal year 2011:_____.

Statement for Joint Committee Hearing
Subcommittees on
Strategic Forces and Seapower and Projection Forces
28 January 2014
Robert L. Butterworth
President, Aries Analytics, Inc.

Chairman Rogers, Chairman Forbes, Ranking Member McIntyre, and Ranking Member Cooper:

Thank you for convening this hearing. We need a lot more attention to this problem to help shape our judgments about what to do. The topic is very important, the facts of the matter at hand are debated, and the consequences of the various approaches before us are neither clear nor guaranteed.

China's Need for Counterspace

China is a large, growing, militarily and economically strong, assertive power, and it has gone to war to expand its control over contiguous regions at least four times since the Korean War.[i] It might well have done so again in its recent disputes with Vietnam, Korea, Japan, the Philippines, and Taiwan, except that its demands now involve a region of national security interest to the United States and US allies. China is not yet ready for a military confrontation with the United States.

If things go well that confrontation may never occur. But China does seem determined to prepare for one as it seeks to exert unilateral authority over an ever-expanding neighborhood. A bellwether here is China's experimentation with counterspace operations. Deprived of reliable and timely space support, US force movements would be slower and less coordinated, its longer-range weapons less responsive and less accurate, its tactical operations in general less focused and more costly, and its global awareness more myopic and less timely.

China's counterspace efforts leaped to world attention in January 2007 with its notorious demonstration of direct ascent/hit-to-kill technology. It is surely looking at other approaches, too, including other kinetic energy weapons, lasers, jammers, and cyber tools to attack data and command and control systems. For the near term, at least, it will probably favor systems to achieve a mission kill by attacking US satellites directly, from orbit or from the ground. The effects of other attacks, on ground stations and data streams, for example, at present seem less assured, owing for example to redundant communications pathways, mobile facilities for command and control, direct downlink options, cyber defenses, and advanced inertial guidance devices in terrestrial weapons.

Developing a means to attack a satellite is one effort; discovering which satellite to attack is another. Trying to link specific satellites to particular military effects can be challenging. (The US faces the same problem itself in deciding what kind of protection to provide for which satellites.) Few satellites are single function, and terrestrial forces might find effective substitutes for lost space support.

I expect targeting is a problem, perhaps *the* problem, that will be addressed using the sort of capabilities for precision orbital and proximity operations that China demonstrated a few months ago. Such operations could help China characterize the US space architecture, as part of China's intelligence preparation of the battlefield, and sensors placed close to US satellites could provide clues about the how, what, and when of the satellites' use for military operations. If so, more extensive examination and operational probes can be expected.

US Planning

The United States, meanwhile, seems still to be without a strategic view of how to help China become a constructive partner in the world community. Was the debris-generating ASAT shot the warning of a bully? A plea for a space arms control agreement? Evidence of a rogue PLA? Is the assertion of control over previously open international airspace (and now backed with military threats) an appeal for the just recognition of legitimate claims? Would acceding to China's actions nourish peace or invite further international extortion?

The perspective offered here is that the US and China are in a long-term military competition which includes a significant effort in space. This competition is not a policy of momentary advantage or transient appeal, and it creates a core issue of national security between China and the United States. It is about, and will require, real capabilities. Finding ways to negate the US military space advantage is a compelling strategic requirement for China, the pursuit of which shows no signs of being moderated by the Defense Department's proselytizing of space "norms" or "deterrence by demarche" or the European Union's struggle to write a Code of Conduct for good guys in space.

Further, the competition is less about space as such than about advantage in the joint fight, the contribution of space to US combat capability. The US National Space Policy issued in 2010 recognized this element, emphasizing the need to assure that functions essential to military operations were provided across the conflict spectrum. Those capabilities might be found in new weapons, tactics, or cyber operations, as well as in space protection. (It appears from public documents that the Space Protection Program of the Defense and Intelligence Community would determine priorities on a different basis. The caution here is that trying to protect most satellites from most threats is a quick path to the wrong side of a cost-imposing strategy.)

The United States has much to do if it is to compete effectively. We need experiments, demonstrations, and exercises that more realistically test our forces' abilities to detect, attribute, and respond to attacks on our space systems. We need to develop, execute, and repeatedly test plans for operations when space is contested, particularly for power projection. We need to coordinate developing and planning for space defenses. We need to assess the cost-effectiveness of selected alternatives to space support. And I hope that we can further integrate space into the joint fight by coupling space programs more closely with other force development activities, including advanced development programs and "lessons learned" reviews.

At the same time we need to ensure that essential space-based support for US military operations will be sustained as long as needed. In previous decades space protection confronted the argument that a dollar spent on protection was a dollar lost to mission performance. Today it seems likely that without protection there will be no mission performance. We might complicate China's targeting problems by exploiting deficiencies in its Space Object Surveillance and Identification (SOSI) capabilities, the sensors used on earth and in orbit to detect and track potential targets. We might do more to harden satellite subsystems to resist thermal and electronic attacks. And we might find ways to engage and defeat an attacker's weapons before they engage their target, our satellite.

Conclusion

None of this is meant to suggest that war with China is inevitable. It does suggest that a good way to help China join and strengthen the existing international order is to be prepared to maintain American principles militarily, including in space.

---

[i] Channel Islands, 1958; Indian Border, 1962; Ussuri River, 1969; Vietnam, 1979.

Robert L. Butterworth
Aries Analytics, Inc.

Dr. Butterworth is President of Aries Analytics, Inc., and principal investigator for the company's national security research, specializing in strategic space and nuclear force issues.

His government service includes a recent HQE appointment as Chief, Strategic Planning, Policy, and Doctrine for Air Force Space Command. Earlier he worked on defense and intelligence programs in the White House, the U.S. Senate, and the Department of Defense. Prior to joining the government, he was an Associate Professor on the tenured faculty of Pennsylvania State University, teaching and conducting research in international relations, national security policy, and research methods.

He is the author of several contributions to basic and applied research in international affairs and national security studies, and has provided Congressional testimony on space policy issues. He has taught courses in space policy as a visiting faculty member at the Air War College and in defense and industrial policy as an adjunct professor at George Washington University.

DISCLOSURE FORM FOR WITNESSES
CONCERNING FEDERAL CONTRACT AND GRANT INFORMATION

INSTRUCTION TO WITNESSES: Rule 11, clause 2(g)(5), of the Rules of the U.S. House of Representatives for the 113th Congress requires nongovernmental witnesses appearing before House committees to include in their written statements a curriculum vitae and a disclosure of the amount and source of any federal contracts or grants (including subcontracts and subgrants) received during the current and two previous fiscal years either by the witness or by an entity represented by the witness. This form is intended to assist witnesses appearing before the House Committee on Armed Services in complying with the House rule. Please note that a copy of these statements, with appropriate redactions to protect the witness's personal privacy (including home address and phone number) will be made publicly available in electronic form not later than one day after the witness's appearance before the committee.

Witness name: <u>Robert L. Butterworth</u>

Capacity in which appearing: (check one)

__X_Individual

____Representative

If appearing in a representative capacity, name of the company, association or other entity being represented:

FISCAL YEAR 2013

federal grant(s) / contracts	federal agency	dollar value	subject(s) of contract or grant

FISCAL YEAR 2012

federal grant(s) / contracts	federal agency	dollar value	subject(s) of contract or grant

FISCAL YEAR 2011

Federal grant(s) / contracts	federal agency	dollar value	subject(s) of contract or grant

Federal Contract Information: If you or the entity you represent before the Committee on Armed Services has contracts (including subcontracts) with the federal government, please provide the following information:

Number of contracts (including subcontracts) with the federal government:

        Current fiscal year (2013):_2_____;
        Fiscal year 2012:_____2_____;
        Fiscal year 2011:_____2_____.

Federal agencies with which federal contracts are held:

        Current fiscal year (2013):_Aerospace Corporation, Institute for Defense
            Analysis_____;
        Fiscal year 2012:___same_____;
        Fiscal year 2011:___same_____.

List of subjects of federal contract(s) (for example, ship construction, aircraft parts manufacturing, software design, force structure consultant, architecture & engineering services, etc.):

        Current fiscal year (2013):___Space and Strategic forces
            consulting_____;
        Fiscal year 2012:_____Same_____;
        Fiscal year 2011:_____Same_____.

Aggregate dollar value of federal contracts held:

        Current fiscal year (2013):___$180,000_____;
        Fiscal year 2012:_____$180,000_____;
        Fiscal year 2011:_____$180,000_____.

Federal Grant Information: If you or the entity you represent before the Committee on Armed Services has grants (including subgrants) with the federal government, please provide the following information:

Number of grants (including subgrants) with the federal government:

     Current fiscal year (2013):_____;
     Fiscal year 2012:_____;
     Fiscal year 2011:_____.

Federal agencies with which federal grants are held:

     Current fiscal year (2013):_____;
     Fiscal year 2012:_____;
     Fiscal year 2011:_____.

List of subjects of federal grants(s) (for example, materials research, sociological study, software design, etc.):

     Current fiscal year (2013):_____;
     Fiscal year 2012:_____;
     Fiscal year 2011:_____.

Aggregate dollar value of federal grants held:

     Current fiscal year (2013):_____;
     Fiscal year 2012:_____;
     Fiscal year 2011:_____.

PROMOTING US NATIONAL AND ECONOMIC SECURITY INTERESTS IN SPACE

Testimony by Michael Krepon

Co-founder, the Stimson Center

Director, Stimson's Space Security Program

House Armed Services Committee

Subcommittee on Strategic Forces

January 28, 2014

Chairman Rogers, Ranking Minority Member Cooper, Members of this Subcommittee: Thank you for inviting me to offer my personal views on how best to safeguard US national and economic security interests in space.

The challenge of deterring attacks on US space assets and supporting infrastructure is not new. We faced this challenge during the Cold War against a very powerful ideological and geopolitical foe. The United States and the Soviet Union fought through proxies and experienced intense crises. We engaged in conventional and nuclear arms races, as well as a space race. And yet, anti-satellite (ASAT) weapons were tested infrequently and both Superpowers refrained from stationing weapons in space. Despite many predictions that warfare to seize the high ground in space was inevitable -- and despite the absence of meaningful trade or financial relations to moderate the Superpower competition -- warfare in space was avoided.

Why did deterrence of space warfare work during the Cold War? One reason was that national leaders figured out that conflict in space couldn't be fire-walled against uncontrolled escalation and warfare in other domains – including the potential use of nuclear weapons. Another reason was that military technologies and delivery vehicles designed for other purposes could readily be re-purposed for space warfare, if the need arose. Everyone understood that counter-space capabilities were a fact of life, even if they weren't often demonstrated. A third reason was that satellites were vulnerable, and that even great additional expense could not alter this fact, except at thin margins.

Vulnerability plus an inferred capability to inflict great damage helped avoid warfare in space.

Now fast forward to a rising China which is investing in space capabilities across the board – including capabilities to damage US satellites. In some ways, it's harder to deal with a rising power than a peer. Communication channels with China are unsatisfactory, and we're not sure if Beijing will approach these issues in the same way that Moscow did back then. Some US analysts have warned of a "Space Pearl Harbor," just as some warned of a "bolt-out-of-the-blue" nuclear attack during the Cold War. What is the best strategy for the United States to continue to rely on the national security and economic benefits that derive from satellites and to deter worst cases? I will suggest a multi-layered approach that involves several common sense components.

Several key conditions that led to the absence of warfare in space during the Cold War still apply today. The possibility of uncontrolled escalation, the vulnerability of satellites, and the means to damage them haven't gone away. If anything, satellite vulnerability and damage potential are greater now than during the Cold War. In addition, there is another factor that could help restrain reckless activities in space: a mutual dependence on international trade and finance between the United States and China that was absent between the United States and the Soviet Union. Plus, as China's military dependency on space grows, its vulnerabilities in this domain will also grow.

These factors could result in the avoidance of a space war with China -- but the United States can't rely on them. If we can't take responsible Chinese behavior in space for granted, how might we influence Beijing's national calculus?

Greater resiliency in space assets can help deter some types of interference, but nothing can protect satellites from a determined, capable attacker willing to suffer the consequences. We can spend money to try to make satellites less vulnerable to some kinds of disruption. But other methods of protection will not be cost-effective, practical or successful.

We can add to dissuasion through disaggregation. Because satellites will remain vulnerable and targetable, it makes more sense to have a greater number of satellites providing repetitive coverage than to rely on a small number of extraordinarily expensive satellites. Deterrence of attack is increased by complicating the plans of the attacker.

Deterrence also rests on knowing the state of play, receiving timely warning of troubling developments, interpreting intelligence and warning signs correctly, and taking appropriate measures to avoid being greatly disadvantaged. In other words, deterrence rests on space situational awareness (SSA). If funding and capabilities for SSA are declining, then the basis for deterring hostile acts and responding to them appropriately could also decline -- even when other elements of a multi-layered strategy are in place. Deterrence of hostile acts in space, as with nuclear deterrence, also rests on secure retaliatory capabilities sufficient to deny advantages to an attacker, as well as effective command and control mechanisms.

Does deterrence of warfare in space, as with nuclear deterrence, also require a dedicated force of ASAT interceptors that are repeatedly flight-tested and ready for use on very short notice? The historical record suggest otherwise. Latent counter-space capabilities point to the same answer.

There are already many ways for major powers to interfere with, damage, or destroy satellites and space-supporting infrastructure, including the use of jammers, lasers, cyber, ballistic missile defense interceptors, and various kinds of missiles. When so much latent capability exists to mess with satellites and infrastructure, dedicated capabilities can be unnecessarily costly and redundant. The testing and use of certain types of ASAT weapons – those with indiscriminate and long-lasting effects -- would be particularly damaging to US national and economic security interests. Because the testing or use of these weapons threatens every nation that relies on space, there is a potential basis to reach tacit or other kinds of agreements controlling them.

Take, for example, nuclear testing in the atmosphere. In 1962, a single, powerful US test damaged or destroyed perhaps six satellites. Not all of them were ours. One was Telstar – the satellite that sparked great public excitement and a hit instrumental record. Kinetic energy ASAT tests can also have indiscriminate, long-lasting effects. In 2007, China tested hit-to-kill ASAT technology against one of its satellites, creating a mutating debris field that continues to pose threats to a great many satellites and human spaceflight – theirs, ours, everyone's. A treaty is in place that bans atmospheric nuclear tests. A proposed international Code of Conduct for space, which I will turn to next, would help establish a norm against testing ASATs that generate lethal, long-lasting debris fields.

We learned during the Cold War that threatening great harm is insufficient for successful deterrence, and that chances of success are greatly improved when diplomacy supplements military capabilities. Nuclear deterrence has been backstopped by treaties. But it's hard to envision treaties banning space warfare, since these capabilities reside in so many military technologies and platforms.

There is, however, still room for diplomacy in a multi-layered strategy to promote US national and economic security interests in space. Deterrence can be strengthened by diplomacy that clarifies differences between responsible and irresponsible behavior in space. Rules of the road do not ensure responsible behavior, but without rules, there are no rule-breakers. Rules of the road can also facilitate appropriate responses to rule breakers. Washington and Moscow have codes of conduct and rules of the road for our navies, armies and air forces operating in close proximity. But there is no comparable agreement for space.

The United States, the European Union, Japan and other countries are working on draft language for an international Code of Conduct for responsible space-faring nations. China and Russia prefer to negotiate an unverifiable treaty filled with loopholes. Last fall, they agreed to a space Code of Conduct in principle, but have yet to sign on to the current draft.

To conclude, there are many layers to a common sense strategy that can help deter hostile actions against US space capabilities. They include the ability to respond appropriately to attacks on US space assets, greater resilience and redundancy, better space situational awareness, improved command, control, and intelligence capabilities, and sound diplomatic initiatives. This multi-layered approach can continue to be as successful today as it was during the Cold War.

Michael Krepon

Co-Founder/Senior Associate

Michael Krepon is co-founder of Stimson and director of the South Asia and Space Security programs.

He has championed confidence-building and nuclear risk-reduction measures between India and Pakistan, several of which have subsequently been implemented. He has mentored more than seventy visiting fellows from the region, and has worked on the general outlines of a Kashmir settlement.

Krepon is the author or editor of thirteen books, and more than 350 articles. Prior to co-founding Stimson, he worked at the Carnegie Endowment for International Peace, the U.S. Arms Control and Disarmament Agency during the Carter administration, and in the U.S. House of Representatives, assisting Congressman Norm Dicks.

Krepon's current research focus is on nuclear stability and crisis management in South Asia. His work on space security centers around the promotion of a code of conduct for responsible space-faring nations, which has subsequently been endorsed by the European Union and the Obama administration.

Krepon received an M.A. from the School of Advanced International Studies at Johns Hopkins University and a B.A. from Franklin & Marshall College. He also studied Arabic at the American University in Cairo, Egypt.

DISCLOSURE FORM FOR WITNESSES
CONCERNING FEDERAL CONTRACT AND GRANT INFORMATION

INSTRUCTION TO WITNESSES: Rule 11, clause 2(g)(5), of the Rules of the U.S. House of Representatives for the 113th Congress requires nongovernmental witnesses appearing before House committees to include in their written statements a curriculum vitae and a disclosure of the amount and source of any federal contracts or grants (including subcontracts and subgrants) received during the current and two previous fiscal years either by the witness or by an entity represented by the witness. This form is intended to assist witnesses appearing before the House Committee on Armed Services in complying with the House rule. Please note that a copy of these statements, with appropriate redactions to protect the witness's personal privacy (including home address and phone number) will be made publicly available in electronic form not later than one day after the witness's appearance before the committee.

Witness name: <u>Michael Krepon</u>

Capacity in which appearing: (check one)

X Individual

___Representative

If appearing in a representative capacity, name of the company, association or other entity being represented:

FISCAL YEAR 2013

federal grant(s) / contracts	federal agency	dollar value	subject(s) of contract or grant

FISCAL YEAR 2012

federal grant(s) / contracts	federal agency	dollar value	subject(s) of contract or grant

FISCAL YEAR 2011

Federal grant(s) / contracts	federal agency	dollar value	subject(s) of contract or grant

Federal Contract Information: If you or the entity you represent before the Committee on Armed Services has contracts (including subcontracts) with the federal government, please provide the following information:

Number of contracts (including subcontracts) with the federal government:

      Current fiscal year (2013):_____;
      Fiscal year 2012:_____;
      Fiscal year 2011:_____.

Federal agencies with which federal contracts are held:

      Current fiscal year (2013):_____;
      Fiscal year 2012:_____;
      Fiscal year 2011:_____.

List of subjects of federal contract(s) (for example, ship construction, aircraft parts manufacturing, software design, force structure consultant, architecture & engineering services, etc.):

      Current fiscal year (2013):_____;
      Fiscal year 2012:_____;
      Fiscal year 2011:_____.

Aggregate dollar value of federal contracts held:

      Current fiscal year (2013):_____;
      Fiscal year 2012:_____;
      Fiscal year 2011:_____.

Federal Grant Information: If you or the entity you represent before the Committee on Armed Services has grants (including subgrants) with the federal government, please provide the following information:

Number of grants (including subgrants) with the federal government:

      Current fiscal year (2013):_____;
      Fiscal year 2012:_____;
      Fiscal year 2011:_____.

Federal agencies with which federal grants are held:

      Current fiscal year (2013):_____;
      Fiscal year 2012:_____;
      Fiscal year 2011:_____.

List of subjects of federal grants(s) (for example, materials research, sociological study, software design, etc.):

      Current fiscal year (2013):_____;
      Fiscal year 2012:_____;
      Fiscal year 2011:_____.

Aggregate dollar value of federal grants held:

      Current fiscal year (2013):_____;
      Fiscal year 2012:_____;
      Fiscal year 2011:_____.

QUESTIONS SUBMITTED BY MEMBERS POST HEARING

JANUARY 28, 2014

QUESTIONS SUBMITTED BY MR. FORBES

Mr. FORBES. The U.S. has changed its attitudes to the Space Code of Conduct over the last several years: from opposition or benign neglect to a stated willingness to engage in conversations. Has the space environment changed for the better that U.S. participation is warranted? Will the Space Code of Conduct deliver on what is our principal objective: a space environment free of threats to our U.S. national security?

Dr. TELLIS. The Space Code of Conduct cannot—and will not—deliver on the principal U.S. objective of preserving a space environment free of threats to U.S. space systems. The U.S. attitude to the Code of Conduct has indeed varied over the years, but that is more because of differences in attitudes between different administrations in Washington and not because the Code itself has become more effective in protecting American interests. The Code must be understood for what it is: it is a confidence-building measure at best. It will not prevent states from developing counterspace programs nor can it prevent any state from mounting counterspace operations against the United States during a crisis or in war. The Code, therefore, cannot eliminate the most serious dangers to U.S. space systems. If successful, the best the Code can do is to restrain states from engaging in kinetic anti-satellite tests that are debris-generating in peacetime: while this would be an important achievement, it is more likely that any such restraint—if it materializes—would ensue because it advances the national interests of the various spacefaring powers rather than because of their formal adherence to the Code per se. In any event, the issue of whether the United States should be an adherent to the Code must be assessed on whether the Code in its totality advances U.S. space interests. Even the most current version of the Code does not unambiguously advance that objective yet. Consequently, the United States should stay involved in the discussions on the Code, but not commit to adhering to it just yet.

Mr. FORBES. How aggressive is China pursuing counterspace technology that would put at risk the open and peaceful use of space? What insight do we have into their intent for developing such technology? What motivates them, and what would de-motivate them in this pursuit?

Dr. TELLIS. China today has the most aggressive counterspace program of any state in the international system. The principal target of this counterspace program is, first and foremost, the United States. The motivations animating the Chinese counterspace program are simple: China views the possibility of a conflict with the United States as serious, and is preparing a variety of military capabilities to deal with that contingency. It has a healthy appreciation of U.S. military superiority and seeks ways to mitigate America's operational advantages across the board. China's counterspace program is part and parcel of this effort. Given China's larger geopolitical interests, there is no way to induce Beijing to forego its counterspace investments. Consequently, the United States must ensure that no matter what China's counterspace capabilities may be, U.S. military operations can nonetheless be successfully prosecuted in every scenario of relevance to American interests.

Mr. FORBES. The U.S. has changed its attitudes to the Space Code of Conduct over the last several years: from opposition or benign neglect to a stated willingness to engage in conversations. Has the space environment changed for the better that U.S. participation is warranted? Will the Space Code of Conduct deliver on what is our principal objective: a space environment free of threats to our U.S. national security?

Dr. BUTTERWORTH. The space environment has not changed for the better, and the Code will not help reduce space threats to our national security. Chinese military space R&D and deployments are particularly vigorous and clearly aimed at degrading the effectiveness of U.S. national security systems.

The most effective measures toward keeping space safe and secure for the benefit of all continue to be led by the United States, working through United Nations committees, alliances, and bilateral agreements, and providing conjunction analysis and collision warnings pro bono to government and commercial space operators around the world.

The Space Code of Conduct offers no practical support for the United States' efforts and could prove diplomatically troublesome. The Code is silent about important definitions and any procedures for monitoring, verification, and sanctions; it calls for sharing information about national security strategies and programs; it calls for complying with and promoting a treaty the U.S. Senate refused to ratify; and as an excuse for the dangerous deficiencies in its drafting, it declares that it is not legally binding.

And in any event, the Code would address less than half of the world's orbital launch activity. Three of the countries on record as opposing the Code (Russia, China, and India) accounted for 48 of the 78 successful space launches to orbit in 2013.

Mr. FORBES. How aggressive is China pursuing counterspace technology that would put at risk the open and peaceful use of space? What insight do we have into their intent for developing such technology? What motivates them, and what would de-motivate them in this pursuit?

Dr. BUTTERWORTH. China's counterspace programs are energetic and diverse because they are critical to China's hopes for being able to challenge U.S. interests militarily. China clearly appreciates the significance of space systems to U.S. military power projection and so is driven to develop effective counterspace capabilities. Most recently in the South and East China Seas, China has been using implied military threats to assert unilateral prerogatives in areas of concern to the U.S. and its allies and partners. China cannot be de-motivated in this pursuit so long as it continues to use military threats to change international norms, practices, and procedures.

Mr. FORBES. The U.S. has changed its attitudes to the Space Code of Conduct over the last several years: from opposition or benign neglect to a stated willingness to engage in conversations. Has the space environment changed for the better that U.S. participation is warranted? Will the Space Code of Conduct deliver on what is our principal objective: a space environment free of threats to our U.S. national security?

Mr. KREPON. The George W. Bush was not enthusiastic about an international code of conduct for space-faring nations. It placed a high priority on freedom of action and wished to avoid any diplomatic undertakings in this domain. This view became harder to sustain after the PLA's 2007 "hit-to-kill" ASAT test, which produced the worst man-made debris consequences since the Space Age began. After this test, some rethinking appeared warranted about rules of the road to set norms of responsible behavior in space—especially regarding ASAT tests that produce mutating, long-lasting debris fields.

Presidential candidate Barack Obama held a positive view about a properly crafted code of conduct for space-faring nations, but his administration moved very deliberately on this initiative. Other issues had a higher priority, and the executive branch and the Pentagon undertook lengthy reviews on how a properly crafted code of conduct might affect U.S. national and economic security. After these reviews were completed, the administration announced that it could support a properly crafted code of conduct. The administration has been very involved in the drafting process led by the European Union. But this process is also going slowly. Progress has been made, but three key hold-outs remain: China, Russia, and India.

In my view, the space environment will become more hostile to spacecraft and human spaceflight as long as the potential for debris proliferation is greater than the potential for debris mitigation. Debris is lethal and does not respect the nationality of spacecraft or manned spaceflight. We face the real potential that some heavily trafficked orbits could become dead zones as a result on debris hits with pinball effects, just as some locations at sea are dead fishery zones. A code of conduct for space could help prevent this outcome by establishing a norm against "hit-to-kill" ASAT tests.

Backers of a space code of conduct can't promise "a space environment free of threats to our U.S. national security." Even with a well-designed code, U.S. satellites will continue to be vulnerable requiring, as I testified, multi-layered deterrence whether or not this diplomatic initiative succeeds.

Mr. FORBES. How aggressive is China pursuing counterspace technology that would put at risk the open and peaceful use of space? What insight do we have into their intent for developing such technology? What motivates them, and what would de-motivate them in this pursuit?

Mr. KREPON. According to published reports, the PLA is testing capabilities and practicing techniques that could be applied against satellites. These capabilities are not unique to China; all major space-faring nations, including the United States, can be expected to possess them. When any country tests such capabilities, others might infer hostile intent, or preparations to be ready to employ these techniques in the event of authorization to engage in warfare. Or they might serve deterrent purposes. Or these practices might suggest, in China's case, a perceived need to play catch-up ball. I am not a China scholar, so I am not well versed enough to hazard a guess about which of these possible motivations, or which combination of motivations, applies.

QUESTIONS SUBMITTED BY MR. ROGERS

Mr. ROGERS. How does the U.S. deter China from entering a conflict in space?

Dr. TELLIS. The best way for the United States to deter China from expanding a conflict to space would be to invest in maintaining all the necessary warfighting capabilities that (i) promise to inflict greater pain on China than would be suffered by the United States in any space war; and (ii) permit the U.S. military to secure its operational objectives terrestrially despite any counterspace operations that may be mounted by China. In other words, the best deterrence strategy is one where the United States clearly demonstrates that it has both the capability and the willingness to run any space-relevant offence-defense arms race provoked by China—and win.

Mr. ROGERS. What are the national security implications if our military lost access to space capabilities in a conflict with the People's Republic of China? Beyond national security, if a system such as Global Positioning System (GPS) was threatened, what would be the potential economic and civil impact on the United States?

Dr. TELLIS. I think it would be safe to say—as a first cut—that the loss of U.S. space capabilities to China in a conflict would be simply catastrophic to the United States. There is no other national military that relies on space for its operational effectiveness as much as the U.S. military. Nor is there any other society that relies on space for its economic wellbeing as much as the United States. The loss of U.S. access to space for both military and civilian endeavors would, therefore, be calamitous. Given this fact, it is unfortunate that we still do not have a comprehensive understanding of what exactly would entail operationally if the U.S. military were to lose access to space in a conflict with China. I believe that assessments of this kind are just beginning and it will probably be a while before they are complete.

Mr. ROGERS. What steps is China taking to increase their Space Situational Awareness (SSA)? What are the risks of this, and what role will their SSA ability play in their counterspace systems?

Dr. TELLIS. China is beginning to build the foundations for a comprehensive Space Situational Awareness (SSA) capability. In recent years, Beijing has embarked on a variety of technical investments to detect and track orbital bodies passing over China through the use of specialized optical telescopes and theodolites, laser satellite-tracking devices such as rangefinders, large phased-array radars, various ground- and space-based signals intelligence systems, and radars associated with surface-to-air missile systems, all of which are capable of searching, acquiring, tracking and classifying objects of interest to Chinese strategic planners. China has also sought to collaborate with various international research organizations, particularly in Europe and Asia, to identify U.S. space systems that are not identified in the open space catalogs maintained by NASA and the U.S. Air Force Space Command.

The objectives of these activities, in the first instance, consist of denying the United States the targeting data that would enable it to interdict China's land-based strategic nuclear platforms and key elements of its conventional forces. Accurate information about U.S. and third-party space reconnaissance assets and overflight patterns is sought in order to permit Chinese commanders to issue the appropriate notifications to their field components in regard to movement and dispersal operations, which are timed to occur outside the window of observation. The Chinese quest for more accurate SSA, however, is equally driven in the final instance by their desire to nullify American space systems, either kinetically or through soft kills or through informational denial operations: all these objectives require Beijing to first know the capabilities of the U.S. space platforms it seeks to defeat, their orbital parameters and their spatial relationship to other orbiting bodies. The ultimate aim of China's SSA investments, therefore, is to underwrite its larger counterspace ambitions.

Mr. ROGERS. Over the past several years, there has been much discussion on an international agreement for a Space Code of Conduct, to establish "norms and confidence-building-measures" according to its advocates. Do you think the Chinese will sign up to this sort of agreement? And if they do, do you think they will stop their counterspace program because of the agreement?

Dr. TELLIS. It is not clear right now whether China will sign on to any Space Code of Conduct, although Beijing has agreed recently—after many years of opposition—to join in discussions of a Code. Even if China were to adhere to any future Code of Conduct, it will not terminate its counterspace programs, which are driven by strategic necessities that transcend the requirements of public diplomacy.

Mr. ROGERS. Please describe the leadership of the Chinese space program, and the relationship between the military and civilian elements. What are the risks of U.S. cooperation with China's civil space program? Please describe the extent of efforts by the Chinese to illegally acquire U.S. technology.

Dr. TELLIS. It must be remembered that China's space program is a remarkably integrated effort. Unlike the United States, for example, where a significant divide exists between civilian and military space activities, and where diversity, heterogeneity, and atomistic competition are the norm in both realms, civilian and military space programs in China are not only centrally directed but are also mutually reinforcing by design. Although specific activities in the Chinese space program may be biased towards civilian or defense applications, the entire enterprise, strictly speaking, is a strategic program with no firewalls whatsoever between the civilian and the military. This "unity-in-difference," centered on the primacy of military considerations which suffuse even the scientific, domestic, and commercial elements of the space effort, is protected at the programmatic level by the organizational structure of the Chinese system. China's State Council oversees the Ministry of Industry and Information Technology, the State Owned Assets Supervision and Administration Commission, and the Ministry of Science and Technology, which through different lines of control oversee the research academies and the defense industry groupings that produce the various technologies for either the People's Liberation Army (through the General Armaments Department (GAD)) or the various ministries that use space products and services. The links between military and civilian space are, therefore, far more robust than often appear in organizational charts.

In this context, the China National Space Administration, which is sometimes depicted as China's National Aeronautics and Space Administration (NASA), is essentially a civilian front for international cooperation and a liaison between the military and Chinese defense industry. The military interests of the Chinese state in the space program are thus affirmatively protected, even though Chinese policymakers rarely, if ever, own up to the military dimensions of their space endeavors. As Kevin Pollpeter summarized it succinctly, "China's space program is inherently military in nature ... Indeed, China's space program is a military-civilian joint venture in which the military develops and operates its satellites and runs its infrastructure, including China's launch sites and satellite operations center." The policy consequence of this fact, from an American perspective, is that any collaboration with China's "civilian" space program inevitably ends up aiding its military.

Mr. ROGERS. How does the U.S. deter China from entering a conflict in space?

Dr. BUTTERWORTH. For China, conflict with the U.S. in space is about military advantage on earth. Space systems are plainly an integral and crucial element of American military power, especially projection power, which is why China is working hard at counterspace capabilities. But for the same reason, the U.S. response to an attack on its space systems would not be limited to counterattacks in space but would reasonably include targeting facilities that housed, enabled, or facilitated the counterspace attacks. That is, the importance of space support to U.S. military operations is both why China would attack in space and why the conflict could not be confined to space.

Consequently, to deter China from a conflict in space is to deter China from a terrestrial conflict with the U.S., a calculation that includes assessments of American projection power, regional military balances, alliances, partnerships, and other "whole of government" considerations. The United States wants to help China become a constructive partner in the community of nations, but doing so apparently will first require denying China any benefits from bullying its neighbors.

Mr. ROGERS. What are the national security implications if our military lost access to space capabilities in a conflict with the People's Republic of China? Beyond national security, if a system such as Global Positioning System (GPS) was threatened, what would be the potential economic and civil impact on the United States?

Dr. BUTTERWORTH. Bluntly, if we lose space we do not play. Space provides the warp and weft of the highly integrated forces we bring to the joint fight. Without space, the battle team unravels, and the separate threads more easily broken.

The economic and civil effects of a loss of GPS on the U.S. are also incalculable, primarily because of the widespread dependence on the timing signal. Navigation is important but probably accounts for about one-seventh of the usage of GPS. Broader losses would come from the loss of timing for the internet, for commercial transactions, for digital communications, and many other elements of our infrastructure.

Mr. ROGERS. What steps is China taking to increase their Space Situational Awareness (SSA)? What are the risks of this, and what role will their SSA ability play in their counterspace systems?

Dr. BUTTERWORTH. China is developing and conducting on-orbit demonstrations of satellites and satellite control techniques that can be used for an intelligence preparation of the space battlefield. China evidently hopes to gain substantial insight into the U.S. "space order of battle" by using sensors to detect and track satellites from various positions in orbit, and by using close proximity operations to refine estimates of the function and purpose of satellites in orbit. The results could provide China a guide to which U.S. satellites to attack, when, and in what fashion to best complicate different phases of U.S. terrestrial operations.

Mr. ROGERS. Over the past several years, there has been much discussion on an international agreement for a Space Code of Conduct, to establish "norms and confidence-building-measures" according to its advocates. Do you think the Chinese will sign up to this sort of agreement? And if they do, do you think they will stop their counterspace program because of the agreement?

Dr. BUTTERWORTH. China has repeatedly said that it is opposed to the European/Space Code of Conduct because China wants an international agreement about weapons in space, while the Code focuses on debris (for which adequate international fora have been in operation for several years).

China has proposed negotiating an agreement that would prohibit placing weapons in space but has insisted that such an agreement would not prohibit ground-based anti-satellite weapons.

China's counterspace program is rooted in China's determination to achieve sufficient military power to be able to win a regional military confrontation with the United States. China will not stop its counterspace program unless it turns to established diplomatic procedures for resolving disputes peacefully and abandons its military bullying.

Mr. ROGERS. Please describe the leadership of the Chinese space program, and the relationship between the military and civilian elements. What are the risks of U.S. cooperation with China's civil space program? Please describe the extent of efforts by the Chinese to illegally acquire U.S. technology.

Dr. BUTTERWORTH. Detailed insights into leadership of the Chinese space program and the relationship between the military and civilian elements can be provided by China experts such as Dean Cheng, and they can certainly help the U.S. understand some of the background of Chinese actions. But regardless of whether an event resulted from military arrogance or civilian impotence, the Chinese government must be held responsible for its actions.

Chinese efforts to acquire U.S. technology illegally include the traditional panoply of technical means together with extensive contacts with Americans in various meetings and circumstances. One area of worry for space operations is ensuring the integrity and security of components and subsystems, including computer chips.

Mr. ROGERS. How does the U.S. deter China from entering a conflict in space?

Mr. KREPON. As noted in my testimony, by a multilayered approach that includes the ability to cause significant harm to a potential attacker, whether in space or elsewhere; by having space situational awareness so as to learn as quickly as possible about potential attacks and to determine the perpetrator; by disaggregating and diversifying our capabilities in space; and by increasing protective measures for satellites when they are cost-effective at the margin.

Mr. ROGERS. What are the national security implications if our military lost access to space capabilities in a conflict with the People's Republic of China? Beyond national security, if a system such as Global Positioning System (GPS) was threatened, what would be the potential economic and civil impact on the United States?

Mr. KREPON. This scenario—what some have characterized as a "space Pearl Harbor"—would place the United States at a profound disadvantage, unless the United States retained the ability and will to retaliate in ways that also placed China at a similar or worse disadvantage. I would expect this to be the case.

Mr. ROGERS. What steps is China taking to increase their Space Situational Awareness (SSA)? What are the risks of this, and what role will their SSA ability play in their counterspace systems?

Mr. KREPON. China's space situational awareness lags well behind that of the United States. Indeed, I believe that the United States has provided conjunction warnings to China when one of its satellites or space missions might be imperiled by debris that we can track better than they—including debris generated by the PLA's 2007 ASAT test. The asymmetry of SSA capabilities would place China at a disadvantage in the event of warfare in space, and would pose the question to China's leadership of whether limited or all-out counter-space attacks would be worth the risk. Improved U.S. space situational awareness would reinforce deterrence against surprise attacks.

Mr. ROGERS. Over the past several years, there has been much discussion on an international agreement for a Space Code of Conduct, to establish "norms and confidence-building-measures" according to its advocates. Do you think the Chinese will sign up to this sort of agreement? And if they do, do you think they will stop their counterspace program because of the agreement?

Mr. KREPON. The Chinese leadership's position is evolving. Initially, Beijing and Moscow rejected a code of conduct, insisting on an unverifiable and ambitious treaty to ban some kinds of space warfare, but not the counter-space capabilities they are developing. Last fall, Beijing and Moscow endorsed in principle the notion of a code of conduct, but not the draft code developed by the European Union. Beijing and Moscow have agreed that some types of transparency and confidence-building measures could have utility, and they have enumerated a number of useful measures that could be incorporated into an international code of conduct They have also stated that a code of conduct should be an interim step to an ambitious treaty that, in my view, is unlikely to be negotiated.

The realization of a properly crafted space code of conduct will depend on several conditions, including the acceptance by China and Russia of pragmatic and useful "rules of the road" for space—including consultative measures and the end of ASAT testing that causes long-lived space debris.

A code of conduct would not stop the development of counter-space capabilities, because such capabilities reside in technologies that could have peaceful as well as malign purposes. Consequently, whether or not an international space code of conduct is finalized, I do not foresee the United States getting out of the counter-space business. Nor would it be wise to do so.

Mr. ROGERS. Please describe the leadership of the Chinese space program, and the relationship between the military and civilian elements. What are the risks of U.S. cooperation with China's civil space program? Please describe the extent of efforts by the Chinese to illegally acquire U.S. technology.

Mr. KREPON. A subsidiary reason why I support negotiations on an international space code of conduct is to learn more about civil-military relations in China as they apply to space. I know very little about how well Chinese leaders have familiarized themselves with the PLA's plans or understand the consequences of their military's doctrine, test practices and exercises. I presume that the PLA briefed the Party leadership about its counter-space programs prior to the 2007 ASAT test that endangered over 200 satellites and manned space programs—including their own. But I don't know whether the Party leadership received a detailed preview of the 2007 test, and whether they knew enough to ask about the debris consequences of this test. I do know that the Foreign Ministry remained silent for two weeks after this ASAT test.

The advent of an international code of conduct for responsible space-faring nations could prompt more internal and international consultations on these matters.

As for civil space cooperation with China, the risks of possible technology loss have to weighed against potential gains from cooperation. I recall that there was considerable anxiety to the Nixon administration's 1972 agreement with the Soviet Union to a docking mission for the Apollo and Soyuz spacecraft. In retrospect, these anxieties proved to be unwarranted. Cooperation between Washington and Moscow in space continues on a daily basis on the International Space Station—despite many other difficulties the United States faces with Russia.

I am a supporter of exploring ways for the United States to cooperate with China in space, without compromising sensitive technologies. I believe that the Congressional prohibition of bilateral engagements between NASA and its Chinese counterpart is unwise.

————

QUESTIONS SUBMITTED BY MR. CARSON

Mr. CARSON. How quickly are we able to reconstitute capabilities like GPS or communications networks if one or more of our satellites was destroyed or otherwise taken offline? In your opinion, are additional investments necessary to increase this pace? If so, which investments?

Dr. TELLIS. In general, the U.S. capability to reconstitute its space-based communications satellites and the GPS system is a function of their orbital altitudes, the character of an adversary attack, and the availability of ready spares and rapid launch capabilities in the United States. A more careful modeling of these factors is essential before your question can be answered satisfactorily. In general, however,

I would say the following: One, the United States must move with alacrity to develop a rapid launch capability, which we still don't have. There are several new private sector solutions that are innovative and possible cheaper, which ought to be investigated. Two, we need to reassess the need and the number of satellites spares for high priority operations, and to provide the budgetary support for maintaining the requisite spares inventory. Three, the most likely threats to our space systems will be less kinetic destruction and more suppression of links that transmit their data; dealing with this challenge is more complicated because its requires multiple and distributed solutions.

Mr. CARSON. Can you describe how increased transparency into counterspace capabilities has impacted the perception of hosting military payloads among commercial satellite operators? What steps can we take to reassure concerned commercial operators of the safety of their satellites? Additionally, what can we do to expand hosted payload opportunities?

Dr. TELLIS. As far as I can tell, most commercial satellite operators still operate on the presumption that space will continue to remain a protected sanctuary, at least as far as commercial systems are concerned. They are more concerned about congestion, debris, and peacetime management of space assets than military interference per se. Obviously, this will change over time, particularly if countries like China and Russia demonstrate a willingness to interfere with commercial systems. The dangers to commercial systems, however, pose new challenges to space deterrence. One approach to these dangers would be for the United States to adopt a clear declaratory policy that treats threats to space systems owned and operated by U.S. commercial entities similarly to those facing U.S. military systems. Another important complement will require expanding U.S. space situational awareness capabilities to encompass critical U.S.-owned and operated commercial satellites as well. Solutions of this sort will be essential as commercial space systems increasingly support U.S. defense operations.

Mr. CARSON. How quickly are we able to reconstitute capabilities like GPS or communications networks if one or more of our satellites was destroyed or otherwise taken offline? In your opinion, are additional investments necessary to increase this pace? If so, which investments?

Dr. BUTTERWORTH. The GPS constellation includes some satellites that can be used as on-orbit spares, and so reconstitution can be quick if not too many satellites are taken offline. In my opinion, it would be prudent to invest in a backup terrestrial system (e-loran) to ensure continuity of the timing signal, vital to so many operations in our infrastructure.

Communications networks can be reorganized fairly quickly in most cases of military need, but doing so would be done based on priority and the overall capacity of the network would be reduced if one of our satellites were destroyed or taken offline. The U.S. military has always needed more communications capacity for its operations. One idea to provide surge communications for regional military operations involves launching perhaps six small satellites with UHF payloads into an appropriately angled molniya orbits. Additional options will become available as the national security community moves further toward data-centric approaches to communicating information.

Mr. CARSON. Can you describe how increased transparency into counterspace capabilities has impacted the perception of hosting military payloads among commercial satellite operators? What steps can we take to reassure concerned commercial operators of the safety of their satellites? Additionally, what can we do to expand hosted payload opportunities?

Dr. BUTTERWORTH. While hosting military payloads might draw hostile attention to a commercial satellite, I have not seen serious concern by commercial operators about becoming a target for counterspace threats. For now, at least, the industry seems eager to offer hosting services for military communications systems that might be involved in "disaggregation."

The primary difficulty with attracting more hosts for military payloads is the incompatibility between the government's acquisition process and the commercial operator's business-driven schedule. The opportunities for hosted payloads will expand, I think, if the Defense Department can provide its payloads to the commercial operator with the agreed technical interfaces and within the commercial operators' production-to-launch schedule (say, 30 months).

Mr. CARSON. How quickly are we able to reconstitute capabilities like GPS or communications networks if one or more of our satellites was destroyed or otherwise taken offline? In your opinion, are additional investments necessary to increase this pace? If so, which investments?

Mr. KREPON. U.S. launch capabilities are diversifying, which is a very positive development. However, certain satellites are harder to replace than others, and my sense is that the United States cannot depend on prompt reconstitution in some, if not most cases. I suspect these conditions also apply elsewhere. I think that everyone on our panel of witnesses has reached the conclusion that, because essential satellites are also vulnerable, resilient, disaggregated capabilities make more sense than relying on very few, highly capable satellites. If disaggregation results in some loss of high-end capability, I would still advocate disaggregation.

Mr. CARSON. Can you describe how increased transparency into counterspace capabilities has impacted the perception of hosting military payloads among commercial satellite operators? What steps can we take to reassure concerned commercial operators of the safety of their satellites? Additionally, what can we do to expand hosted payload opportunities?

Mr. KREPON. I am inclined to support hosted payloads because they would result in disaggregation, thereby helping to offset counter-space capabilities. I view this as a cost-effective step that can complicate the plans of a potential attacker, thereby reinforcing deterrence. That said, hosted payloads could still be vulnerable payloads.